A COURSE

in

PROSPERITY

60 days to transform your relationship with
money and prosperity!

JACOB GLASS

DEDICATION AND ACKNOWLEDGEMENT:

For Neville Goddard, Rev. Ike, Stuart Wilde, Catherine Ponder and Raymond Charles Barker.

INTRODUCTION

Greetings and welcome to a Course in Prosperity! I want to begin by acknowledging you for making this wonderful investment in yourself. <u>You are worthy as fuck to have your dreams come true</u> – to be, do and have the life you choose for YOURSELF. And it just may be easier than you think. I suggest you allow the process of increasing your prosperity and living your dreams to be easier than you ever thought it could be. Are you WILLING to LET it be easy and FUN?

You are the authority in your life. You are the chooser. YOU get to DECIDE for yourself how far you want to go in life. There is no God in the sky making choices for you or withholding your good. God is the Universal Presence of YES, fuck YES!

I like to get right down to business, so I'm not going to tell a long story about my past with money and prosperity. Suffice to say I was raised in a lower middle-class family in rural Pennsylvania in a home filled with financial fears and issues – food stamps, repossessed furniture, literally hiding in the house from creditors, changing phone numbers to avoid bill-collectors, many job losses from my father's alcoholism and so on. I grew up with a lot of fear and anxiety around money and survival – plus religious guilt for even thinking about money or wanting to live with nice things and money in the bank.

It took me a very long time to ALLOW myself to prosper, but it doesn't have to be that way. I could've gotten to the prosperous life a LOT sooner if I hadn't taken to many bogus "spiritual" side-trips and delays which were a result of the fucked-up thinking of a world that is the extreme opposite of REAL Spiritual Truth, which is that we are meant to prosper, thrive, and joyously expand ALL through our lives.

This is yet another book in my series of books from my Spirit Guides or Angels. They speak to me daily and I share what I'm told in these books for those who find them helpful. You will probably find some typos and errors here as this is self-published and perfection is not one of my goals in life. If that bothers you, best to not purchase this particular book – but, if what you want is the information and results – read on!

The book begins with what I call "fruitage." We are known by the fruit our lives bear just as a tree is known by the fruit it bears. I am not interested in theory or philosophy but in what bears good fruit. Therefore, the book begins with letters and emails I've received from students and clients of mine who have USED these principles to bear good fruit.

Then, the rest of the book are the 60 daily lessons and mantras (or affirmations) to help guide your mind and consciousness to the place of alignment with the prosperity and abundance that is your Divine Right and Inheritance!

The journey of prospering and thriving is a life-long magical one of self-discovery. You are discovering the God-Source within YOU and how it really is TRUE that it is done unto us as we BELIEVE, not as we wish or hope. Hard work and struggle is NOT necessary but an open heart and mind are extremely necessary in order to truly TRANSFORM our relationship with money, abundance, prosperity, success and knowing that we can be successful AND still be happy, centered, loving and kind.

Please let go of any old cultural think you may have that "rich" successful people are evil and selfish. If you think that "rich" means Ebenezer Scrooge, J. R. Ewing, Alexis Carrington, Mr. Potter from "It's a Wonderful Life" and other such nonsense, then it's time to WAKE UP from that hypnotic spell and realize that if you equate money and success with greed and darkness, you will never allow yourself to have it. HERE is where the healing begins – in the mind. The real purpose of this book is the healing and transformation of the mind.

A Few Notes/Tips/Suggestions:

1. Get a journal or notebook to use for writing out the mantras you enjoy most and to make up your own.

2. Make a section of your journal the "Fruitage " section where you record your own prosperity results as you go along. Include every penny your find, every gift you receive, every single thing that tells you that this shit works (or #TSW as we do in my groups and classes). The more you gather up evidence that you are increasing your prosperity consciousness, the more it will increase!

3. Don't merely read the daily entry, SAY THE MANTRA OUT LOUD with FEELING. Repeat it to yourself throughout the day. I strongly suggest you write it out by hand SEVEN TIMES. The subconscious mind learns through repetition and FEELING.

4. You may want to tear out the page with the Prosperity Creed and tape it to a mirror where you can say it ALOUD WITH FEELING every morning. This is a huge vibration-shifter and can work wonders!

5. In the back of the book there are reading suggestions as well as several pages for note-taking. Check them out as well as my website jacobglass.com. And I would love to hear from you about your fruitage and demonstrations so please email me through my website with yours.

6. Finally, HAVE FUN WITH THIS! The more JOY you have around the process, the more manifestations you will experience!

EPIGRAPH

"The thief, (ego/fear) comes to steal, kill and destroy. I have come that they may have life and may have it more abundantly (to the full, til it overflows)."

- John 10:10

A Course

in

Prosperity

THE PROSPERITY CREED
(SAY THIS ALOUD DAILY FOR THE ENTIRE 60 DAYS)

I SEE AND FEEL MYSELF AS A
VESSEL OF DIVINE LIGHT.
I FORGIVE AND I AM FORGIVEN.
I AM LOVED AND LOVABLE.
I SEE AND FEEL MYSELF
AS WORTHY.
I SEE AND FEEL MYSELF
AS ENOUGH.
I SEE AND FEEL MYSELF
AS POWERFUL AND ABLE.
I SEE AND FEEL MYSELF AS
JOYOUS, PEACEFUL, HEALTHY,
PROSPEROUS, SUCCESSFUL
AND LOVED.

Fruitage Letters/Demonstrations

Rising up to riches

Dear darling Jacob,

This is not merely a delicious fruitage report, it is a love letter to say THANK YOU a thousand times over for being my teacher of teachers, my joy guide and my North star.

In April 2018, I was a newly sober, exhausted Home-health and Hospice nurse, scrimping along in fear and lack with a well-groomed 60-year-old poverty consciousness. Despite my occasional lovely visions, my Course in Miracles studies and classes, I was lost in the throes of my addiction, playing whac-a-mole with my divinity.

My new friend, Jenny (knowing I was open as only connected souls do), sent me a YouTube of you, her spiritual teacher. Within 20 seconds, I knew I had come home. I was gob smacked! Who is this man? How have I missed him all these years? It was game on! I ordered your books, inhaled your YouTubes for hours on end.

On May 1st, per your suggestion, I wrote out my first of many I remember when letters to myself. I wrote *"I remember when I thought I'd never retire and look at me, retired early with tons of money and freedom."* I changed my set-point of consciousness to one of possibility and easy abundance. I began to FEEL free and powerful and divine. I began to wake up every morning with the words thank you on my tongue. I began to expect good things each day. I drew to me three amazing soul sisters and we began a Sunday morning Jacob Joy masterclass on my back porch, and we all began to RISE UP! It was one of the richest times of my life so far.

On September 15th of that year, sweet Pete's father died unexpectedly leaving us a gorgeous inheritance and his adorable little beach house in Long Beach, California. With barely a split second of thought, we looked at each other and said let's do it, let's run through these colorful and playful open doors! I now know, without a shadow of a doubt, that my change in consciousness brought this good to me. I was aligning with this all along.

Through my daily connection and study with you, Jacob, I have learned to live in a state of deep gratitude and of calm delight. I decide now. I choose now to FEEL good. Every step of the road from Seattle to Southern California has been effortless; the loveliest people emerged constantly because I expected them to. Since that first I remember when letter to myself, I've written countless more... all of which have come to pass. All of them!

Today, at this very moment, I'm sitting in my beautifully remodeled beach house, the doors are open, the palm trees are swaying, the garden is abloom. And I am shining in my holiness, my joy, DIVINELY CONSCIOUSNESS in this peace.

Every day is a vacation day, every cup of coffee delighted in. I have never felt more alive, dear you.

I love you.
Your forever grateful, coffee table dancing cabaret soul,

Elise B.

A family prospers

Dear Jacob,

When I first started listening to your talks, my husband and I were living paycheck to paycheck and had over $80,000 in debt. I was always stressed and worried about money. From listening to your talks, I learned about tithing and the spiritual principles around prosperity. I started practicing these principles faithfully and went "all-in". I tithed regularly, studied your books and talks, practiced feeling rich, and more. My prosperity consciousness grew, and my situation just kept getting better and better in ways I never could have guessed. For one thing, money was ALWAYS coming in, and always from such surprising sources! A relative would drop by with an inheritance from years ago we didn't know we had; I would win contests I didn't remember entering; I would receive a refund for something I had forgotten about; a stranger in a grocery line would turn around and hand me a gift card for no reason; all of these things happened and more.

These principles are true, and they work no matter what is going on in the world. In 2020, during the pandemic and a time of financial uncertainty for so many, my husband got his biggest promotion to date and a huge raise plus several bonuses. We became debt free for the first time in our marriage and are now in the best financial position we have ever been in. I continue to practice these principles and won't ever stop.

I am teaching my children these principles as well, and it is awesome seeing how it works for everyone, regardless of age, circumstance, or worldly condition! I love hearing my kids declare, "mom, I got another check today; I'm such a money magnet!" I am so thankful for Jacob's teachings and love seeing how great life can get.... because it just keeps getting better!!!!

Sincerely,
Jill M.

Happy and healthy

Dear Jacob,

The better it gets, the better it gets. Who knew that my life would benefit in such a significant way?! I went in, eyes wide open. Not only because I think you're the best teacher of the 21st century (no hyperbole here) but because you, by example and word, help people mine their lives for the great stuff.

I follow your teaching because it's such a beautiful upward spiral and happy journey. That alone makes it worth the time. But also, because it just feels SO damn good. And, as you know..."*nothing is more important than that we feel good!*" You just do that for people, while their lives, as a result, get better.

I came into this Masterclass with a good, happy life and came out with so many marked demonstrations that it can't be denied that they were a direct result of this series. I went deep; finally took responsibility for the good things that happened in my life; practiced imagining in a way I'd never done before; amped up my gratitude; reframed my definition of myself and claimed, with confidence, my Source within. What happened next? The horrible asthma I had been experiencing? Poof, gone. My husband, who hadn't worked in years, got a directing gig. I was able to replace my 16-year-old Acura with a new Tesla; and all of a sudden I realized that I was no longer living paycheck to paycheck, and I had a nice savings account to boot. How did that happen? It was like magic, but not. The external changes just reflected the internal changes, which made it seem like magic. It was you teaching us that daily, consistent and persistent work (drip, drip, drip) would affect our subconscious minds to erode old beliefs. It works!

#TSW! I also love the way the daily practices have shifted my habitual, erroneous thoughts to be automatically questioned. Thoughts like, 'I'll never and it's too late,' are quickly counteracted by, "The only thing true is woman sitting in chair' and 'all is well' and one of my favorites, 'it's okay, it's okay, it's okay.' How soothing and healing. My self-talk has changed. It is joyful and cathartic work that makes me happy in my now, eager for more.

So, thank you. I love you. I'm so grateful that you live the life and career you've chosen with such joie de vivre ;). You help me, and countless others, do the same.

With the utmost gratitude,
Zan

<u>Changing beliefs creates prosperity</u>

Dear Jacob,

I want to share the fruitage I have experienced since I found your teachings and ministry 2 years ago. I have read all your books, listen to your services twice a week along with receiving daily upliftment from your blog and Instagram postings. All this exposure to your teachings dripped, dripped, dripped its way into my subconscious and as a result, my beliefs about myself changed in a couple of key areas.

For the first time, I was able to allow myself to want what I wanted, instead of tempering my desires with what I thought I could afford. Once I was open to wanting what I wanted, I had an insight to calculate how much that lifestyle would cost and then to obtain the money for that lifestyle. I calculated that I needed to make $10K more a year to afford that lifestyle. I remember that you had said a few times that there is someone doing the exact same job you are doing and make much more money. This inspired me to conduct a job search which resulted in manifesting a job during the corona virus pandemic making $22K more a year. And it looks like I am in line with getting a $5K to $10K bonus at the end of the year.

This allowed me to move into the apartment of my dreams which I truly deserve. My complex is only four years old, so everything is state of the art and the complex backs up to the beautiful Catalina mountains. The apartment ticks off everything on my list: Lots of light, open floor plan, kitchen island, washer and dryer in unit, granite counters, stainless steel appliances, friendly neighbors and located in the lovely Oro Valley neighborhood. Oro Valley is a suburb of Tucson, so I am a desert dweller just like you!

Thank you so much for speaking your truth and sharing it with us. My life keeps improving and I look forward to seeing you in person at one of the do-it-yourself retreats you will be giving in Palm Springs!

Love and appreciation,
Barbara Maxwell

Becoming a DOER

I first started going to hear Jacob speak in the Park Suites Hotel in San Diego sometime around 2010. I was in my early 20's at the time and remember being inspired by his candid approach to spirituality and humor but I absolutely fell into the category of, "I'm just here for the entertainment". I would pop-in from time to time with my favorite Starbucks just as one might go see a fun movie. I didn't read any of the books or do the work and thus of course, didn't have any of the results other than feeling really lovely for the rest of the day after hearing him talk.

It wasn't until 2015 and the pains and discomforts of my life (finance, romance, health & career) had escalated to a level that I decided to become slightly more committed, and you know, actually do some of the things he recommended. I started listening to his recorded lectures on my hours-long commute each day, writing down what I thought at the time were total cringe worthy Money Magic Mantras and putting them where I could see them, and doing his visualizations pretty consistently. Over and over again, I'd hear him recommend this "Dear Jacob Letter" until one day I actually decided to write one.

I pulled out my iPhone Notes and started to write a letter that felt so fabulous to write but also a little far-fetched and woo-woo. It was the solution to all my most pressing pains and problems as if they'd already been solved, which all at the time seemed impossible or at the very least all things that would be incredibly difficult and take a lot of effort by me or 100 years to happen.

Dear Jacob,

I'm writing to give you a really exciting update. My boyfriend resolved all his tax issues with the IRS and is back to working full-time in his business. It's been so helpful for us, and our relationship has improved so much. It's also so amazing that I'm a perfect size 6 (perfect for me) and I've lost about 50 pounds without even trying. I feel so great in my body! Oh, and not to mention we own the most amazing home now. The ceilings are so high and it's so light and bright and beautiful and it even has a yard. I've paid off all my debt and it allows me to really enjoy my life and our new home together. My new boss is amazing, and I love working for her. There's so much love and happiness in my life. I'm so grateful.

I read the letter to myself almost every day for about a month. And then, I stopped doing it on a regular basis and then forgot about it altogether.

It wasn't until recently that I found that note again. I was searching for something else and in January of 2020 found that note on my phone I had written to Jacob 5 years before.

I read that letter, sitting on a couch in my custom-built dream home with tall ceilings and the most amazing natural light. I read that letter back sitting next to my now fiancé who received a waiver because of a statute of limitations from the IRS for over 200k of debt and was able to resume his profession, which helps our family so much. I read back that letter sitting in my size 6 jeans after losing over 75 pounds without even trying after getting a bacteria in Costa Rica and rebuilding my relationship with food. I read that letter after paying off all my debt - sitting in a home that had so much love, happiness and the freedom I had only dreamed about. Not to mention, I had a new boss who is quite literally the best.

I read back that letter and I said out loud "Oh my God, this shit works doesn't it".

It was a timely find as it reconnected me to my daily dose of Jacob and his series of Masterclasses that literally saved my ass and helped me thrive during the pandemic - when I most certainly would've lost my shit without a daily commitment to these tools.

Doing the things activates the fruitage but I'm not sure I would've found these principles, especially so young, if it wasn't for Jacob.

I will be forever grateful for you. I've written a new Dear Jacob Letter and I simply can't wait to really send it to you.

Gabrielle

Allowing ease creates prosperity

I've been on a JOURNEY the last 30 years of my life, and, since I started really working from and with PRINCIPLE a few years ago, thanks to you, I am finally gently going down the stream, merrily, merrily, merrily. Life is really but a dream.

Because of my background as a psychotherapist, and having done a lot of my own therapy and self-help work, I was so used to looking for the source of all issues and fixing it. Boy, I did a lot of fixing. And hustling! I hustled for love, for work, and for money. It never failed that every time I took matters into my own hands, I got stressed out, picked the wrong guys, and lost money. Got involved with a married man, and gave him lots of advice about saving his own marriage. Did I mention I was a psychotherapist? lol! Put my apartment on Airbnb, even though that's, ya know, illegal. Became embroiled in a 6-year lawsuit with an ex-boyfriend in Argentina, which just siphoned money from me, year after year, UNTIL...I started really putting PRINCIPLE to work by trusting the Universe, aka Tom Ford, my uber classy Cosmic Concierge, Intergalactic Lawyer, Extraterrestrial Agent, and Super heroic Life Office Manager, to take care of my shit for me. All I had to do was, as you have always said, "SHOW UP, PREPARED, ON TIME, DOING WHAT I SAID I WOULD DO WITH A GOOD ATTITUDE." Life just got so much easier. AND more prosperous:

After giving up on my search for an investment property several times because things were way out of my price range, I ended up buying a wonderful condo in Palm Springs, and paid cash for it. Palm Springs wasn't even on my radar, as it wasn't a place I frequented. Turns out, it's my other staycay favorite, along with the Central Coast. This investment is making me a nice chunk of change to circulate for bills and just the fun things in life for me and my husband! And we get to stay there for free and let our friends stay, when it's available.

After having had enough of living in our overpriced apartment with noisy neighbors, homeless people, sneaking into our building, and police coming over to deal with resident altercations, I made it very clear to the Universe what I was looking for. 2 months before lockdown, we moved into a BIGGER apartment in a better area of the valley in a smaller complex, just down the street from a homeless-free park, where I would feel safer walking our dogs. While I am certain we would have made the higher rent, it was such a blessing for us to pay less for our quieter pad.

The Pandemic was the busiest I've ever been acting-wise. I do a lot of stage work, and there I was creating a community of actors around the country to read plays on Zoom--a program I hadn't even known about, but which I mastered easily very early during shut-down--and casting all of us in parts we normally wouldn't be cast in. I also got a paid directing and hosting gig, and a play I wrote was accepted into a development program. Being on lockdown gave me the ability to learn producing, casting, directing, and new technology, AND people took notice, which is leading to more opportunities, now that things are opening up. I didn't do anything out of fear that I would lose industry connections. I just did it because I wanted to continue practicing, and because it was fun! I also got a very featured part in an Apple+ show, sitting next to two, popular, mega stars on camera. How? Because I wanted bigger and better roles, stated it, and released the how to the Universe.

When I lost a condo rental client that booked for 2 months earlier this year, I was a little worried, but then released it and trusted the Universe, thinking...Oh, well, I'll just enjoy it with my family! A week later, I got a SIX-month rental!

My years-long lawsuit over some property with my ex-boyfriend was finally settled, once I handed it over to the Universe and trusted it would be handled in a win-win scenario. I had no idea how, because this thing had dragged out for so long. I had faith that the money owed was NOT MY SOURCE, but that GOD IS MY SOURCE, and rested in that. Then one day, I got a call from my lawyers in Argentina, saying I had to fly out there in less than 2 weeks to sign the papers, because the other party finally settled. The call came just a day or two before I wrapped my latest theater project, and I was on the plane to collect my cash a few days later. My lawyer said that if I hadn't made it, I would have lost the case and the money owed me. Boom! Divine timing!

Another thing Principle has really helped with is just having a happier, healthy marriage and friendships. Relationships are SO much EASIER, now that I continue to release people to their own good and to remember that they have their own relationship to Source. Now, reunions are more peaceful, when I accept who they are, where they are, and leave the rest to them.

Most recently, I totaled my car in an accident at the top of the year, and I was totally stressed out about it. Unfortunately, it was my fault, but I kept treating and blessing the other party in my mind, and releasing it to Tom Ford to fix. I was looking at a possible extended battle with some very aggressive lawyers and a higher car payment for a replacement car. But I made clear what I wanted--an electric car with accessible payments-

-and GOT IT around $200 a month LESS than my other car and with more advanced technology. WHAT? (We were planning to refinance the old one before the accident, but kept procrastinating, for some reason. Universe was, like, "FINE, I will take care of that shit for you, since you can't seem to handle it." I also got to use a loaner car for free, while waiting for my new car to be delivered. Then the other party settled within 3 months, which, my lawyers and my insurance company mentioned, was really unexpected. Unexpected? HA! Easy peasy for my Cosmic Concierge!

Jacob, there are countless other things that have happened, as you know--free gifts, surprise money, computer upgrades, parking spots, compliments galore, money literally floating down the street, where I could see it and pick it up, generous tips, surprise side jobs that are fun, genuine Prada cashmere sweaters for $5, etc.-- that I could have never even imagined manifested, since I started this work. I am truly PROSPEROUS in every way.

Sometimes, I just want to binge all day on a serial killer documentary, or cackle like a fiend, as I scroll through the mean comments on a political post, but, when I do that now, since starting the work, the effects are immediate and physical. I feel and act like a little shithead, and I get a little nauseous and lethargic. But being this sensitive to making negative choices is good, because I always know that I need to recommit to doing the work!

It really works, if you work it, as they say. So grateful to be learning from you and our possum groupies. It just makes me a more joyful person.

Thank you, thank you, thank you -

Evie

Inner Peace Attained

I've been in the plumbing and water works industry since the '80's. After a while, I felt I should be doing something more 'meaningful' and 'worthwhile'. Sharing this with Jacob, he said my work was vital to everyone, and without water... we'd be back in the Dark Ages in a short period of time. Certainly not experiencing life as we know it today. He said I should consider my work as a Ministry. And I did. Things got much better, I felt more valuable and aligned...As though I had a calling. I approached my work with a different attitude. It was easier to go to work. I felt useful. I also realized this was an opportunity to make good connections with people. And standing for good quality, honesty and going the extra distance... proved to be fulfilling, and profitable. *"Show up, on time, doing what I said I would do, with a good attitude."*

This also gave me impetus to start volunteer work for two organizations... raising funds and awareness for people who do not have adequate water supply. I've raised over $25,000 over the years, and alerted people to the population who live each day without adequate water.

I'm glad I went to Jacob for advice here. And indirectly, I think other people are glad, too!
PF

From struggle to peaceful prosperity

I have been contemplating how to articulate the massive and life changing shifts in my life since I started listening to your talks and reading your books.

The outward world may not perceive the changes as radical as I know they are. When I first found you I felt alone, my relationships with my family and parents were very difficult. I was always fighting with my partner. There were alcohol issues as well. We had huge money problems. My job looked sketchy and his business was floundering .

We also struggled with our neighbors! One called the police on us, (the police acknowledged it was nutty). There were property line disputes and blaming for weird things. The other side was worse.

My job did get de-funded, and I was transferred to another job I really didn't like and my boss was unreasonable.

My life was miserable, and it felt like a mess. I remember several times sitting in my car and almost in tears trying a strategy or plan of yours. One time I said ... you know what I am good at, the work I'm meant to do... figure this out. I believe within a week I was approached to change to another division which resulted in a job I loved and grew in! I loved my co-workers and supervisors.

With the neighbor I thought " do I need a lawyer' then used your teaching of forgiveness . This neighbor is now a very good friend who mows our lawn for us!

I know (feel) I have strong supportive friendships with like-minded people. I have an active fun social life.

We no longer have money issues and my relationships with my family are really great!

The proof has come to me most vividly in this way. My daughter, who the first 8+ years in my period as a single mom saw my struggles up close, has on several occasions made statements about my changes. She has remarked how peaceful and happy I seem . After a difficult (covid hospital) situation she later discussed how centered and calm I was able to handle things thru to a positive end. She says and posts things she dismissed years earlier.

You have often spoke of opposite world or how things from the outside may look the same. Same house, same boyfriend, etc. - but how radical the changes are. Yes money (prosperity) has allowed us to build additions or travel, or buy things. But the change is far more profound. I am grateful, daily! that I stumbled across you years ago on the internet. I am grateful for the peace and prosperity that you teach is now mine. My life continues to expand and get better. Miraculously this seems to rub off on those around me as I say and try less. This shit works!!!

Karen

A COURSE
in
PROSPERITY

DAILY
READINGS

DAY 1: I FEEL RICH!

Feeling is the one and only medium through which ideas are
conveyed to the subconscious.
- Neville Goddard

We want you to say this right out loud to yourself - to try it
on for size. Go ahead, say it, "I FEEL RICH!" Say it over
and over again, particularly if it feels awkward, or
uncomfortable, or you have resistance to it. Say it until it
begins to DELIGHT you and gets your energetic valves
opening up so that the LIFE energy can flow through with
ease and increasing speed!

There are multi-millionaires in your culture who FEEL
financially terrified, and who inside are still that child who
wore ratty clothes to school and lived in fear most days
because their needs were barely being met or were not met.
They might not admit it, but they FEEL impoverished much
more than they actually feel rich. Many of them would scoff
if you told them they were rich. They think "those other
people over there" are rich, but not them. But YOU can
FEEL rich even if you don't have a single dime in the bank
and own little more than the clothes on your back. Rich is
NOT a fact, it's a FEELING. Catch the FEELING and you're
already home!

Remember, there is never anyone to convince but yourself -
of anything, really. You are simply convincing your own
subconscious mind to manifest whatever it is that you
WANT to be, do or have. When the subconscious mind is on
board, IT'S A DONE DEAL! You need never "sell" anyone

else on anything ever again. You are only ever selling yourself on what you want - and you don't do it by FORCE or by bullying. The best way to sell anything is through INSPIRING and romancing the subconscious mind - by setting the proper MOOD (FEELING).

It starts here with the word. We can talk and talk to you, but you believe what YOU say far more than what anyone else ever says. If you say you are poor, limited, on a fixed income, too old, too tired, can't do it - so be it. Your subconscious mind will back you up by having you FOCUS on anything that is evidence of THAT. If you begin to say you FEEL RICH over and over and get the FEELING, your subconscious mind will back you up by having you FOCUS on all evidence of THAT. Life is really very simple - you SEE on the outside whatever it is you feel inside.

<u>Money Magic Mantra</u>:

I FEEL RICH!

DAY 2: I SEE AND FEEL MYSELF AS WORTHY!

Your worth is established by God . . . Again, nothing you do or think or wish or make is necessary to establish your worth. This point is not debatable except in delusions.
- A Course in Miracles

This is truly the GOOD NEWS the world should be embracing, but it is extremely difficult for most humans to accept the fact that they are not made worthy or acceptable because of their struggle, achievements and accomplishments. Nor are they "unworthy" for lack of them. The Truth is, you are worthy, lovable and enough simply because you EXIST as an extension of the Divine Mind, the One Source of Life! Even if you feel that you have done nothing with your life and have had one "failure" after another, you are nevertheless whole, complete, batteries included, ready and able to thrive beyond all past precedent without PROVING anything to anyone. NOTHING ever makes you one bit worthier or less worthy. We want you to begin to allow yourself to FEEL that, not merely accept it intellectually. SEE IT AND FEEL IT.

For some of you, this may seem like blasphemy if you have old religious or superstitious thinking. You may still be hypnotized by your culture to think that you must EARN everything - even love, approval and acceptance. #bullshit In fact, it is IMPOSSIBLE to earn these things. They are the gifts of Grace.

You are not too much. You are not too little. You are unique in all of Creation and you need do nothing to puff yourself up or pull yourself back. Let go of the stress of trying to BECOME something or even to BE SOMETHING AND SOMEBODY. Be still. For this moment, let everything fall away as you accept yourself just as you are, and just as you are not. You are not broken, damaged, wounded or empty inside. Those are all lies, lies, lies and illusions. PRACTICE seeing and feeling yourself as worthy and enough. Say it a thousand times a day if necessary. Let yourself marinate in this realization until it goes right down into the marrow of the bones. It is one of the truest things you can ever say about YOU.

Money Magic Mantra:

I SEE and FEEL myself as worthy and enough.

DAY 3: I HAVE A LIMITLESS SOURCE.

Abundance is a natural law of the Universe. The evidence of this law is conclusive; we see it on every hand. Everywhere Nature is lavish, wasteful, extravagant. Nowhere is economy observed in any created thing. Profusion is manifested in everything. The millions and millions of trees and flowers and plants and animals and the vast scheme of reproduction where the process of creating and recreating is forever going on, all indicates the lavishness with which Nature has made provision for man. That there is an abundance for everyone is evident, but that many fail to participate in this abundance is also evident; they have not yet come into a realization of the Universality of all substance, and that mind is the active principle whereby we are related to the things we desire.

- Charles F. Haanel

We want you to create a Prosperity Journal if you have not done so already. In it, you will record ALL your daily demonstrations of abundance and prosperity in whatever forms are revealed to you. It would be best if you can carry it with you and it really should be written out by hand because of how it affects the human brain to actually write something down. You could record them on your phone and then put them in the journal at the end of the day if you like.

Write down every penny you find in the sofa, every gift you receive, including free refills of coffee if that is not usually the policy of the establishment, every bonus, found treasure, every mental, physical or emotional healing (for that is prosperity too). This is like the notebook a detective carries around when gathering up evidence to prove the case. YOU are that detective gathering up the continual mounting evidence that YOU LIVE IN A LAVISH UNIVERSE and are provided for in the most wonderful magical ways that you probably did not notice when you were busy running around like Chicken Little gathering up illusory evidence that the sky is falling!

Already, some of you have been having prosperity demonstrations since starting this journey with Us! Have you been noticing and taking note, or have you been writing them off as "coincidence" while you continue to struggle and worry? Pay attention dear one. YOU are a part of the lavish extravagance of Nature too you know!

<u>Money Magic Mantra</u>:

My Source is lavish, extravagant and
pours out golden blessings to me daily!

DAY 4: I DEFINE MY OWN STANDARD OF PROSPERITY.

I define prosperity as the ability to do what you want to do at the instant you want to do it. Money in the bank is a good idea, and an intelligent life insurance program is wise. Why don't I define prosperity in terms of money? Because prosperity isn't money. Money is necessary for prosperity, and prosperity will produce it, but prosperity is not money. If you are able to do everything you want to do today, and can do it the way you want to do it, you are prosperous. You are as rich as anyone with ten billion dollars.
- Raymond Charles Barker

Your culture is completely insane, and you should not need Us to tell you this for the evidence of it is overwhelming. So why "compare and despair" over the insane toxic concepts and ideas that worldly culture is forever tying to feed you? What that world calls prosperity is often nothing more than bondage and burden. OUR concept of prosperity is FREEDOM, FREEDOM, FREEDOM! It is the freedom to live as YOU choose and to set your OWN standards for EVERYTHING in your life. What then would be the point of trying to impress the peanut gallery or get the approval of a single living soul other than your own? No point at all.

No one owns anything in the physical anyhow - not even your own body. It belongs to the physical as part of this temp assignment of joyous expansion, and when this incarnation is done, you will turn it in along with every other physical thing.

If you want to have cars and boats and mansions, that is your business. If you want to live in a tiny cabin in the mountains, so be it. If you want to travel the world on a private jet, fine. If you want to never leave the farm, what of it? YOU ARE THE CHOOSER. And you can also change your mind as many times as. you like. Yes, keep your agreements or renegotiate them, but do not make the mistake of living a life by the standards of a world culture that is mentally ill and vicious.

YOU are creating YOUR OWN world, remember? All humans do whether they know it or not. Why create one that pleases everyone but yourself? STOP "looking" at the picture of how things appear, and start tuning in to see how they FEEL to YOU. Then, if you do not like how they feel, either change them, or change your attitude about them - or both.

How would you choose to live if you did not give a rip what anyone else (in your past, present or future) thought about it or about you?

Money Magic Mantra:

I am choosing to create my own reality
and to live by my own standards.

DAY 5: MY THOUGHTS BECOME THINGS.

There is a thinking stuff from which all things are made, and which, in its original state, permeates, penetrates, and fills the interspaces of the universe. A thought, in this substance, produces the thing that is imaged by the thought. One can form things from their thought, and, by impressing this thought upon Formless Substance, can cause the thing thought about to be created.
- Wallace D. Wattles

Everything in your world begins with thought. As you look at the world around you, there is nothing that did not come from thought at some level - whether the thought of a human or of the Prime Creator. Nothing is random. What you give feeling-backed thought or attention to, comes into form, whether physical form or a powerful thought form. And though you may think of thought forms as some nebulous unimportant "thing," let Us assure you that for most humans, their thoughts are more real than a physical object that fell on their foot and broke it. This is why it is so important to know that you are not your thoughts, that thoughts are not personal, and therefore you can change them and choose new ones and eliminate old ones as you please! But it does take practice and consistency.

Take a few moments to reflect right now on the thoughts you have been entertaining the past day or so. You may want to write them down on paper. Now, without judging them at all, simply look to see how each of these thoughts FEELS. There is no need to label them as positive or negative or good or bad. Simply notice how each one FEELS to YOU. Without guilt, blame or shame, ask yourself whether the thought is helping or hindering you, whether you want to keep it or not, whether you would like to see it manifest in YOUR world. Then, choose to eliminate some and to keep some and let yourself be inspired and uplifted to even expand to NEW life-giving thoughts.

It's a very fun game to play and as you continue to improve you can win some very wonderful prizes as. your thoughts turn to things!

Money Magic Mantra:

I love choosing thoughts that FEEL good to ME!

DAY 6: MONEY LOVES TO BE WITH ME.

In the psychic area of life, money is a person. Money has a
mentality. Money has emotions. Money has feelings, and if
you hurt the feelings of money, she is going to stay away
from you, or give you trouble, or both. You may personify
money to yourself however you like - perhaps as a very
sensitive and desirable man. Whichever way you personify
money, if you start dealing with money on that basis, you
will get a lot more money a lot faster!
- Reverend Ike

Everything physical is still made up of whirling swirling
ENERGY - the EXACT same energy. The energy itself is
neutral. What you do with it is what gives it meaning. "I
have given everything I see in this room all the meaning that
it has for me" A Course in Miracles reminds you. There is
nothing wrong with loving money any more than it would be
wrong to love a hummingbird, a crystal, a book, or a
gardenia. It's the SAME ENERGY in different forms.

And that energy is RESPONDING TO YOU. If you hate and
fear money, it will hate and fear you right back. There is
nothing going on outside of your own consciousness. If you
hate the industry you are in, it will hate you right back. If
you love the town you are in, it will love you right back. You
may not be loved or hated back in exactly the SAME WAY,
but life will continue to reflect your own consciousness back
to you. It is Law.

We know this may be pushing some of the buttons of you
more "spiritual" types, but that's only because you have

those big honking buttons right out front where they get pushed and keep you stuck in poverty thinking. Those are the buttons that have got to go!

<u>Money Magic Mantra</u>:

I love money and money loves me!

Day 7: I'VE DECIDED TO THRIVE!

What you decide with the conscious mind is produced by the
subconscious mind. If you fail to decide an issue
consciously, your subconscious takes the accumulated
decisions of your years of living and produces an experience
like unto them. It then produces under a law of averages.
There are too many average people, who let this law of
averages operate them. Life requires decision as well as
desire. Unless you exercise the spiritual gifts of desire plus
decision, you will remain an ineffective person.
- Raymond Charles Barker

Far too many spiritual types are simply overly passive
wishy-washy wishers and hopers. Consequently, they tend to
live lives of "same old, same old, same old" because they are
not actually making decisions or being proactive in their own
lives. They think it is "spiritual" to consult a thousand things
outside of them, waiting for "a power greater than
themselves" to send them a sign of what to do or to lead
them to the open door. That would be like sitting in a dark
room for 10 years waiting for Something to give you a
mystical sign to get up off your ass and turn on the lamp!

Use the GPS analogy here. You don't sit in the garage in
your car waiting for the GPS to give a sign of where you
might like to go today. YOU must DECIDE and then
PROGRAM the GPS, and even THEN it will not help you
until YOU put the car in drive and step on the accelerator to
feed the engine some gas. THEN, the GPS will kick in to
say, "*Please proceed to the highlighted route and the route*

guidance will start." YOU ARE THE DRIVER. YOU ARE THE CHOOSER.

Guidance kicks in AFTER YOU make your decision. Wishing and hoping are stupid and useless wastes of time. Daydreaming is a very high vibration use of your time IF you allow it to lead you to actually MAKING DECISIONS, even though you have no idea HOW it will all happen. You may have no idea HOW the GPS in your car is going to get you to your destination, but YOU are still the one who has to SET the goal - YOU DECIDE on the where, it knows the WAY.

Desiring to prosper, to be healthy, to have more love in your life, to be happier - that is step one. But desiring without decisions will quickly move you into the category of wishy-washy wisher and hoper who life passes by. YES, you must even DECIDE to be happy. It's not random. It's not luck. It's not genetic. It's a DECISION. Choose the what, take a step forward, the Guidance will kick in very quickly. *"A journey of 1,000 miles begins with a single step."* Lao Tzu

<u>Money Magic Mantra</u>:

I've DECIDED to prosper and thrive!

FINANCIAL FLOW MONEY
MAGIC MANTRA:

MY MONEY REPLENISHES ITSELF

CONTINUALLY AND SWIFTLY.

MY ACCOUNTS ARE ALWAYS

FILLING UP AND OVERFLOWING.

I EASILY PAY OFF

MY DEBTS EVERY MONTH,

PAY ALL MY BILLS AND TAXES,

AND HAVE PLENTY OF MONEY LEFT OVER

FOR SAVING, INVESTING

AND TO PLAY WITH.

MY INCOME IS CONSTANTLY INCREASING.

MONEY IS FUN FOR ME AND IS

AN ALLY IN CREATING THE LIFE I CHOOSE.

DAY 8: INSPIRED ACTION IS FUN!

We strain too much for our demonstrations. A demonstration is nothing less than the simple fact that through some action in your own mind upon the Cosmos, which provides the inevitable necessity of a different reaction from the Cosmos and the Law of Mind in action, ideas are brought into play and made manifest in our experience that were not there before, or made better than they were before. This is done without helping or pushing the ideas along. This is the only way a demonstration is made, and is the only way we can know that we have made one.

- Ernest Holmes

Human strain in demonstrating comes from TRYING, forcing, manipulating, controlling, and getting into the HOW instead of rolling in the ecstasy of the WHAT. In other words, NOT BEING RELAXED. Manifestation comes from a RELAXED and RECEPTIVE state of Consciousness. "Let go, let go, let go, let go, let go" is Our favorite mantra to you now.

You would do very well to completely dissolve the notion that you have "needs" and instead declare that you have only "delicious desires." This will help to put you in the playful MOOD and mindset necessary for the most wonderful demonstrations. If you must try, try softer rather than trying harder. The harder you try, the more you activate resistance and the worse it all gets.

Yes, We urge you to make decisions, to be proactive, to promote the ideas that you want made manifest in your own world, but that is primarily done on the INNER planes. Remember, you are only ever convincing YOURSELF, not the culture "out there." Your main promoting is to your own subconscious mind, and this must be done in the MOST relaxed state of calm delight and positive expectancy. EXPECT things to work out and to go very well for you. Unclench, unstress, unbutton. THEN, when taking physical action, it will be delicious INSPIRED action and not stressfully trying to MAKE SHIT HAPPEN. "Making it happen" does work beautifully, ON THE INNER PLANE - through gentle happy persistently feeding the ideas to the subconscious mind where She can go to work on them in the most delightful and often effortless ways. Action is FUN when it is done this way, rather than as a "helping" the Source which does not need your help.

<u>Money Magic Mantra</u>:

I relax, tune in and then only take action if it is Divinely Inspired from within. Inspired action is fun for me, and I have no attachment to how it all gets magically worked out. I love taking inspired action!

DAY 9: MY PROSPERITY IS PEACEFUL AND PLENTIFUL.

To yield successfully to the desire as an accomplished fact, you must create a passive state, a kind of reverie or meditative reflection similar to the feeling which precedes sleep. In such a <u>relaxed</u> state the mind is turned from the objective world and easily senses the reality of a subjective state. It is a state in which you are conscious and quite able to move or open your eyes but have no desire to do so.

- Neville Goddard

Brother Neville is describing his particular way of getting into the summoning and receptive mode, but your way may be very different. The IMPORTANT part of this We want to get across to you is the RELAXED part. Nothing is more important than this FEELING of relaxation and calm delight in allowing in your greater and greater good.

Many of you think you must get EXCITED and MOTIVATED in order to have your dreams come true. In fact, the extreme opposite is true. We have witnessed humans being very MOTIVATED and action oriented in MAKING their dreams come true. They are excellent at the summoning part of the equation, but they rarely make it to the finish line of actual completion. They get so close and then it all just disappears like a misty dream they awaken from with a jolt. It is simply because they have been TENSE - some of them for decades. An EXCITED state is rarely a receptive state. In fact, it is often frenetic and repellant.

You need not follow Neville's directions to close your eyes or to be seated or in the supine position. Your eyes may be open as you walk along the beach or clean the house, as long as you are perfectly relaxed as you IMAGINE your desire fulfilled without even knowing how it happened. This may only last for 30 seconds a day. It's not about sustaining it for any period of time really. It is about inner relaxed enjoyment and a NON-ATTACHMENT to the vision. It is not even about faith or belief. Just get into the FEELING of pleasure in the vision itself.

If your dreams are not manifesting even though you are taking inspired action and keep on showing up, prepared, on time, doing YOUR part, it is most likely because you are not relaxed enough to let it in. This is simply fear arising in an untrained mind. For YOU then, the practice of SURRENDER will go a very long way toward the fulfillment of your prosperous visions. It is time to rest in Grace. Slow down your mind. Take beauty walks and cat naps and soothe your way into alignment. True prosperity is not about FORCING the Universe to respond to you. That is a given. It is not about GETTING prosperity. Prosperity is natural, normal, plentiful. Relax and breathe, relax and breathe, relax and breathe. And daydream of anything that FEELS GOOD.

Money Magic Mantra:

I surrender to the calm delight of Source bringing all my dreams to pass in perfect timing and ways as I relax and breathe in Grace.

DAY 10: MONEY IS MY GOOD FRIEND.

You must sell yourself on money as a spiritual idea until it
becomes an automatic subconscious pattern with you.
- Dr. Raymond Charles Barker

We want to keep reminding you that money is every bit as
"spiritual" as crystals, prayer beads, holy books, incense,
candles, mandalas, crucifixes, altars and any other physical
thing you can name. Same, same, same. And many of you
need to FORGIVE money for the many fear and attack
thoughts you have had about it over the years, for you have
believed many ridiculous stories concerning something
which is actually quite neutral. It is only projection which
makes it "bad" or "good." YOU give it all the meaning it has
for you.

Money is simply a means of ENERGY exchange. Money is
energy. And in your culture this is truer than ever for you are
moving further into "contactless" exchange of that money as
it flies through the ethers without you ever putting your
hands on paper or coins. It is the circulating of ENERGY in
order to make your life easier and more comfortable. With
money, you need not create your own electricity to heat and
cool and light your home. With money you need not grow
wheat and harvest it and so on in order to make a loaf of
bread. Money simplifies your life in so many ways and yet
often YOU use it to COMPLICATE things MENTALLY
and EMOTIONALLY.

Money is a spiritual idea because when you see it correctly,
you will treat it with as much kindness and honor as those

crystals, altars, prayer beads and such. It is here to HELP you and it is not hard to get or hard to find. It's flying through the air all around you right now. You simply need to be a welcoming place for it to land! It's like a plane circling the airport waiting for clearance.

Money Magic Mantra:

Money is my good friend, and we love to play together.
Money is fun!

DAY 11: THE LAW OF SATISFACTION PROSPERS ME NOW.

We either make ourselves miserable or we make ourselves strong. The amount of work is the same.
- Carlos Castenada

We cannot remind your often enough that EVERYTHING is energy, energy, energy. Everything is consciousness, consciousness, consciousness. Life is the dance of energy with energy, and YOU are leading the dance. Life simply responds to your lead. Many of the cliches in your world have turned out to be helpful if you look more deeply. When a parent says, "If you don't stop crying I'll give you something to cry about!" they are stating a Universal Principle which reflects this dance of energy. This is how the Universe operates - the better it gets the better it gets, the worse it gets, the worse it gets - according to YOUR lead. If you keep laughing, it will seem as if the Universe keeps giving you something to laugh about. If you are worried, it will seem as if life keeps giving you something to worry about. YOU lead.

The dominant energetic pattern in your particular culture is one of dissatisfaction. The human mind is simply never satisfied and is usually looking at what is wrong, what is missing, what is too much or not enough, what is uncomfortable or MOSTLY what "needs to be fixed." And this keeps bringing more and more of the same.

However, if you will practice what We call "The Law of Satisfaction" you will begin to find more and more and more things to be satisfied and happy about. If you are dissatisfied with your current situation, begin to find ANY positive aspect of it or of ANYTHING that you can focus on and amplify in your energetic field. This will take great discipline in the beginning for many of you, but over time it will become a HABIT that builds momentum.

Perhaps you are afraid that if you become satisfied with your now that things will never "get better" or that you will have a kind of complacency which will keep you "stuck" in some mediocre place or situation. The OPPOSITE is true. The MORE you practice ENERGETIC SATISFACTION, the MORE you will have to be and feel satisfied about. It is Law. What is there to be satisfied about in your present time and place and situation? Beat THAT drum!

<u>Money Magic Mantra</u>:

Right here, right now, I have everything I need to be happy!

DAY 12: I AM FASCINATED BY THE BEST IN LIFE.

The act of taking money out of its "maybe" hazy state is the act of manifestation.
That act is accomplished by observation.
- Stuart Wilde

Whatever you observe with the most INTEREST and FASCINATION in life you will ultimately achieve vibrational harmony with - even if the fascination is one of horror. Do you not know of those who study an illness so long that they eventually come down with it even if it is extremely rare and not contagious? They have achieved vibrational harmony with it in consciousness, and that becomes an alignment in their very cells.

Therefore, you should only be fascinated by your delicious desires and not by anything that you would not want to personally experience. And it doesn't mean running from anything you find unpleasant either. For instance, a medical doctor can be one who is fascinated by illness, or one who is fascinated by health and wholeness. It's about CONSCIOUSNESS and FOCUS. People who are fascinated by their illnesses rarely heal or get much improvement. People who are fascinated by their money problems and issues even while saying they don't want them, rarely prosper and thrive.

CHOOSE what you want to observe, see, notice, amplify, and invite into your life. The 'best in life" is according to YOU, not the culture. Your best in life may be the observance of hummingbirds, gardens, acts of kindness, trips abroad, fashion, art, rivers and mountains - YOU are the chooser of what will fascinate you. And what fascinates you will come to you and roll in ecstasy at your feel like a puppy. Therefore, choose mindfully, carefully, wisely and joyously.

Money Magic Mantra:

I look for the things that delight and fascinate me and they come to me quickly and often!

DAY 13: I AM LETTING SHIT GO!

You have heard it said that Nature abhors a vacuum. It is particularly true in the realm of prosperity . . . If you want great good, greater prosperity in your life, start forming a vacuum to receive it! In other words, get rid of what you don't want to make room for what you do want.
- Catherine Ponder

It is very important to realize that prosperity has nothing to do with "stuff" or in hoarding. People who have a poverty consciousness are scavengers. ANYTHING that is "free" they will accept, whether they can use it, need it, or even like it. This is particularly true of those who grew up with some sense of scarcity. It is the extreme opposite of prosperity. Storage units are almost always a sign of scarcity consciousness - the fear that one cannot create whatever they want or need fresh every moment. This is living on yesterday's manna.

This is not only true in terms of physical "stuff" but in terms of old ideas, beliefs and even relationships that are no longer a vibrational match. Humans often think that they are "too old" to make new friends, so they hold onto dysfunctional relationships which actually only drag them down emotionally, physically and spiritually.

It is very good to be continually CONSCIOUS of what is and isn't serving you by noticing how you FEEL when you think about something or someone, or when you are in their presence. There is no lack of people on your planet. Age is irrelevant. Consciousness is EVERYTHING,

EVERYTHING, EVERYTHING. When We say continually, do not get exhausted at the thought of this continual cleansing process. You brush your teeth every day. You probably wash dishes daily. You get rid of the dust and dirt by cleaning your home regularly. Do not let things build up or pile up. Clean things out on an ongoing continual basis and keep ONLY what serves you in having more joy, peace and love in your life.

Money Magic Mantra:

I deserve the best and I accept the best now. I let go of what no longer serves me to make room for what does.

DAY 14: I LIVE ON A BOUNTIFUL INCOME.

There is an abundance of opportunity for men and women who will go with the current of LIFE and cease swimming against the tide. The law of riches is the same for you as it is for all others. It has been said that the amount of fruit that falls to the ground and rots in the tropics every year would feed the whole world.
Nature is lavish, extravagant, and bountiful.
- Dr. Joseph Murphy

Are you preparing to live on less money in the future or preparing to live on MORE money all the time? What you prepare for is what you are inviting, expecting, and eventually manifesting. Simple cause and effect. So many humans affirm and declare, "I am on a fixed income" and then wonder why they feel so small and limited in what they can be, do and have in life. It is done to them as they believe, affirm and declare.

If your pension, 401K, inheritance, disability check, or ANYTHING of the physical world is your source, then you are already in more trouble than We can possibly begin to tell. But if you know your TRUE LIMITLESS SOURCE then there is no ceiling, no limit, no cap to what can flow to you as you continue to expect and declare joyous expansive increase of good!

Age has nothing to do with it. At all. That is only another belief to be dissolved and neutralized with Truth. Money and resources can flow to anyone at any time from places and people you have never even heard of if you are willing to

OPEN the portals of your PROSPERITY CONSCIOUSNESS and let it in!

Money Magic Mantra:

I am on a bountiful limitless ever-increasing income of delicious dollars and lavish extravagant good!

DAY 15: FORGIVENESS MAKES ME RICH!

Tell me what kind of thoughts you are holding about
yourself and your neighbors, and I can tell you just
what you may expect in the way of health, finances, and
harmony in your home.
- Charles Fillmore, God Will Pay Your Debts, Prosperity

Forgive us our debts, as we forgive our debtors.
Matthew 6:12

To forgive is to cancel the debt. You take it off the books. If
you are in debt and would like to be free, you need to be
doing forgiveness 70 x 7 and more. Forgiveness is the way
to free yourself from indebtedness. That INCLUDES
forgiveness of YOURSELF. Grievances and grudges will
keep you in debt. Learn to let things go quickly and to be
impossible to offend. Do not keep a mental-emotional record
of wrong-doings. Do not feel that others "owe" you
anything. Set all hostages free if you wish to be free of debt.
This includes those of you who have resentments against
"lenders" who you feel took advantage of you when you
were in need. You've got to let that shit go!

We are not saying that you should "write-off" money that
you have loaned others, but it would probably be a great idea
if you did so and it would lift a great burden from you. And
please, you need to keep YOUR agreements to pay others
back whatever you may have borrowed.

Indebtedness is mental bondage and the way to set
YOURSELF free is to forgive others for their "trespasses"
against you and yours. That doesn't mean you like them or

approve of their behavior. It means you "take them off the books" and cancel keeping track of them anymore. Stop looking back. As you learn to "close the books" on all grievances against others and yourself, you will find it much easier to get out of debt and stay out of debt.

Begin by making a list of those you feel "owe you" anything at all - even gratitude or appreciation. Then, "close the books" on it and write "CANCEL" as YOU cancel the debt and release them once and for all. Include yourself by forgiving yourself for any and all financial mistakes and missteps you have made in the past. Keep your agreements, but keep NO grievances, guilt, blame or shame!

<u>Money Magic Mantra:</u>

I forgive quickly and easily and watch my money grow!

DAY 16: I AM OPEN TO RECEIVE!

She had always expected to give but had never expected to
be given to! When she asked what she could do about it, I
said, "That's easy. We will just reverse the thought pattern."
Within a few months she became, and still is, one of the
most successful practitioners we have ever had.
- Ernest Holmes

Prosperity and all good is a matter of YOU being in the
Consciousness which allows it in. You can stop trying to
figure out how to GET your good from other people or
institutions or from some resistant dude in the sky. Use that
same energy to RELAX and adjust your thinking so that
your valves are OPEN to the flow of Source! This is the
reversing of the mental patterns of limitation, struggle,
sacrifice and scarcity.

This is a state We call "positive expectancy." Many humans
are used to the other kind of expectancy - expecting things to
go badly, to not work out, to be troublesome and worrisome,
and so on. We are helping you to reverse all that nonsense.
This is why We will keep reminding you that Nature is
lavish, extravagant and wasteful! Just as you expect the sun
to come up every morning and for you to have enough air to
breathe all day long, you should begin to expect that you will
have what you want and need because that is how the
System was set up from the gate. Only human resistance and
strange beliefs keeps it from being so.

LINE UP and OPEN UP! Line up with your good by EXPECTING it! No one else can line up for you. No one can open your valves but YOU. You're the one. We are here helping you and tuning you all the time, but only to the degree you want and allow. How open are you right now? Remember, open is RELAXED, not excited. RELAXED in calm delight and positive expectancy. And please, SAY these Money Magic Mantras we are giving you each day OUT LOUD! You NEED the vibration of the spoken word to help shift YOUR vibration into the state of OPEN, OPEN, OPEN!

Money Magic Mantra:

Something wonderful and PROSPEROUS is going to happen to me today!

DAY 17: I AM ENOUGH

If you don't respect yourself, it's hard for people to grant you worth, so people will always undervalue you. If, say, you've always felt yourself to be an outcast, you may exclude yourself from the marketplace because you've excluded yourself socially.
- Stuart Wilde

No one can give to you what you are unwilling to give to yourself, no matter how much you may WANT them to. You can only receive what reflects your own consciousness of self-worth. YOU are the one who sets your value in the world. You may THINK it is "them" - those who hire, or who loan, or who seem to have the power and resources. It is not. It is you, every time, no exceptions. As within, so without. This is why We will keep repeating this particular lesson from time to time.

If "they" undervalue you, it is a reflection of how you undervalue yourself. But you can easily reverse that thought pattern with gentle, patient consistency. That is what these writings are all about! We are not fixing you or even summoning more prosperity to you. We are helping YOU to make the changes in your own Consciousness which will LET IN greater and greater and greater good in as many ways as possible that you desire.

It is a STRETCHING exercise. Some days you are tighter than others. Some days you are looser and more ready to extend the stretch. That is not what is important. What makes the difference is showing up every day and doing your best stretch for THAT day. No comparison to past days and no pushing yourself too hard.

Today's lesson may be Our most simple and yet the MOST POWERFUL one of all. You are not saying it to "them" or to the Universe. It must be said BY YOU, TO YOU! We want to ask you to start to become aware of what you are saying TO yourself ABOUT yourself. This is more important than anything anyone else has ever or could ever say about you.

This is why the Mystics' Creed includes this important declaration. Say it often, to yourself, until you believe it with every cell in your body. Your body is listening and responding, as is the entire Cosmos.

Money Magic Mantra:

I am worthy. I am enough.

DAY 18: I AM A MASTER MANIFESTOR.

It is only by a change of consciousness, by actually changing your concept of yourself that you can "build more stately mansions" - the manifestations of higher and higher concepts. (By manifesting is meant experiencing the results of these concepts in your world).
- Neville Goddard

When you are at home, take some time to look around you while you drink in the vision of everything that your gaze falls upon. Look at the lamps, the furniture, the appliances, the personal and sentimental items, and even the things that you think you do not like. Then, take personal responsibility for all of it. Know that YOU manifested ALL of this into your reality, into YOUR world.

We don't mean that you built the lamp or baked the loaf of bread. We mean that YOUR CONSCIOUSNESS brought it into your personal reality. It doesn't matter if your spouse decorated the place, or if your children have filled it with things not to your liking. It doesn't matter if it's a house that was left to you as an inheritance, or if someone else is paying the rent, mortgage and bills. It doesn't matter if it's a hotel room or if you are currently "couch surfing" - it is ALL here IN YOUR EXPERIENCE because it matches YOUR consciousness and therefore YOU manifested it FOR YOURSELF.

In fact, you've been manifesting since before your physical birth. You've always been manifesting based on your consciousness. Therefore, you may not have known it, but you are a MASTER MANIFESTOR! And We want you to realize that the vast vast vast majority of what you have manifested is really very good! Do not let your mind begin to focus on the things that came that you are not so happy with or crazy about, but instead pat yourself on the back for creating a reality in which you have a bed to sleep in, food to eat, people who like or even love you, lamps to light your reading. In fact, pat yourself on the back for manifesting the ability to READ!

Do you see what We are doing here beloved? We are pumping up your concept of YOU! For much of your life you may, as most humans have, simply created by default rather than consciously and deliberately. Too often, people manifest the life they think is possible for them, rather than the one they actually WANT. The process of manifestation is not about creating and attracting the "stuff" - that is simply the icing on the cake. YOUR SELF CONCEPT is the actual delicious cake. You don't live the life you deserve. You live the life you THINK you deserve. Think highly of yourself and it will be reflected in your outer world.

<u>Money Magic Mantra:</u>

I am a master manifestor and I am now deliberately and consciously creating the life I choose. I am worthy to receive and I acknowledge that I have created all the good in my life so far!

Day 19: I assume the best and expect the best.

All transformation begins with an intense, burning desire to
be transformed. The first step in the "renewing of the mind"
is desire. You must want to be different (and intend to be)
before you can begin to change. Then you must make your
future dream a present fact. You do this by assuming the
feeling of your wish fulfilled. An assumption, though false,
if persisted in will harden into fact.
- Neville Goddard

There is no such thing as an objective world. Each one sees
they world she projects and believes in - nothing more and
nothing less. Even those who claim to live only by
SCIENCE and FACTS are deluding themselves for they see
only the "science and facts" that are in basic agreement with
their own consciousness. Everything else gets invalidated,
left out, or is completely invisible to them.

Therefore, it is so IMPORTANT that you always be
DECIDING what you WANT to SEE. Then, you must
assume it is possible, and even more - assume is it
ALREADY THERE. It may still be in the invisible, but this
is exactly how the invisible becomes visible. There is an
inner determination to judge NOT according to appearances.
The only exception to this is when it has to do with the free
will of another person. You must not even attempt to
COMPEL others to do YOUR will for it will backfire in the
most awful ways.

The Law of Assumption here teaches that you are to
ASSUME the very best every day, all day long. Assume that

you are always at the right place at the right time, that things are going to go very well, that you always have what you need, that everything is always magically working out for you, that you have Divine Diplomatic Immunity, that people love you, that money always flows to you in fabulous amounts, that health and vitality are your normal daily state of being, that only good lies before you, and on and on. And as with all of our lessons - this is about progress, not perfection. Simply practice, practice, practice. Practice makes progress.

Money Magic Mantra:

I am receiving all the blessings of Source and the gifts of the Universe today! I am worthy to receive them and am delighted to watch them unfold!

Day 20: Thriving is natural for me.

Prosperity is the circulation of money in your world. It is
movement. It is activity. It is flow. Poverty is the result of
misunderstanding of life. The Universe is crammed with
prosperity. The nation is rich in everything imaginable.
- Dr. Raymond Charles Barker

Yes, prosperity is the circulation of money in YOUR life,
but it is also the circulating of love, peace, joy, harmony,
wonderful relationships, health and vitality, clarity, success
and all that is good! Circulation is LIFE. Congestion is
death. It is natural and normal to have plenty of these in your
life and you can if you will stay focused on continuing on in
the right direction. Each day a step in aligning with the
Spiritual Truth is work well done!

Neutralize and dissolve any and all belief in struggle, lack,
sickness, limitation and sorrow by pouring in Spiritual Truth
in generous doses throughout the day and night - one thought
at a time. You are doing a marvelous job and We are sending
you encouraging messages and signs all the time. Are you
paying attention to see, hear and feel them? Do you sense
Our loving arms around you? Do you see the evidence of
Our love for you as We keep on sending you things that you
love and that are your favorites, or are you lost in worry and
fear thoughts while you walk right past all the delicious
delights We are putting in your pathway?

Don't bother looking harder for them. Instead, look softer.
Look more gently, patiently and kindly. Breathe deeply and
let your body release all tension as you soften your gaze and

align with a Higher Authority and a more oceanic way of seeing, feeling and sensing your world. No need to push or struggle or strain. We are here, We are here, We are here. There is no need for HARD WORK. Let the mind go still now. Be still. Breathe and let go. Turn within. All is very well. This is already a magical day - simply know that things are unfolding perfectly and this is a day of Divine Activity and Right Action because of your Consciousness and not because of your DOING. You are not here to fix anyone, not even yourself. All is well.

Money Magic Mantra:

I always have everything I need to thrive in this moment. I let go and surrender to Divine Love as Grace does all the heavy lifting. There is nothing to fear.

DAY 21: I WRITE MY OWN SCRIPT.

The dramatization of the theme is left to the originality of the second "Mighty One", the author. In dramatizing the theme, the author writes only the last scene of the play - but this scene she writes in detail. The scene must dramatize the desire fulfilled. She mentally constructs as life-like a scene as possible of what she would experience had she realized her desire. When the scene is clearly visualized, the author's work is done.

- Neville Goddard

Perhaps you still have no idea of what a magical creature you are. The air around you fairly crackles with an effervescent unmanifested non-physical energy which is waiting to be turned into things and experiences. And you are doing it ALL the time even though you are mostly not aware that you are. WAKE UP BELOVED! YOU are creating your own reality with this magnificent thinking stuff. Do not let it become manifest through unconscious mental patterns which no longer serve your greater good! Awaken and rejoice that you are NOT a victim of the world you see - you are the creator of it! If you want to SEE a different world, YOU must write the script and play the part!

And as Brother Neville teaches, you do not have to write the whole script or the how of it all. Simply write the final scene of the goal achieved, the desire satiated, the culmination of all good having been accomplished. We are not talking about an "end of life" scene but of all the little scenes of your daily living that concern you in any way and of which you want a happy outcome. Nothing is too small or too large for there is

NO order of difficulty in this. In fact, it needs to BE FUN AND FEEL GOOD in order to work quickly and efficiently. Why would you write a scene you would not ENJOY playing out?

We are going to push some of you here and go a giant leap farther than We have before when We told you that life is not about struggle, sacrifice and HARD WORK. It is actually about PLAY, LAUGHTER and JOY! Now, what is the story you are writing about today?

<u>Money Magic Mantra</u>:

I write only fun "happily ever after" stories for myself
for I am the author of my life!

DAY 22: I NEED FEAR NOTHING.

Retrogression is temporary. The overall direction is one of progress toward the truth.
- A Course in Miracles

You would do very well right now to remind yourselves that you need fear nothing and you need fix nothing. Your job is to breathe and align, breathe and align, breathe and align. You must give up the habit of fighting whatever energies are present and learn to work WITH them. Not every day is about "go, go, go!" And not every good movement is forward.

Instead of fighting, pushing, and fixing, TUNE IN. Remember that to everything there is a season and a time. You have gotten very confused about this is your 24/7 world, which is extremely unnatural. There was time when you could not watch TV or scroll, scroll, scroll the internet all night long. Things of the world would shut down on Sundays and in the wee small hours so that you were forced to STOP. Just STOP. You have experienced this forced stopping in the recent pandemic. But have you gotten the LESSON?

Prosperity is not about money ONLY increasing in your life. It too has energetic cycles. Sometimes there will be more inflow and sometimes more outflow. At other times it will seem like nothing is happening. JUDGE NOT ACCORDING TO APPEARANCES AND ABOVE ALL, FEAR NOT! DO NOT GO INTO RESISTANCE AND FEAR. Tune in. Slow down. Stop the mind from racing and FIXING and fearing. Fear not, be not afraid - of anything.

Some days it will seem as if nothing is moving according to YOUR plan for salvation. Fine. Do NOT push HARDER or you will begin to break things, like your inner peace. Instead, step back, breathe, let go, get calm and SURRENDER the day to Grace to work out - or the week, or the month, or the year. Sometimes the most beneficial movement can be a few steps back rather than forward. Some days the wonderful prosperous thing that happens is that you simply decide not to panic or resist. Some days the prosperous thing that happens is an overflowing sense of inner peace and well-being regardless of what the outer picture looks like.

<u>Money Magic Mantra</u>:

I need fix or fear nothing.
All things are held perfectly in the Hands of Source.

DAY 23: I AM A CENTER OF DIVINE FLOW.

Infinite good is already established within your own consciousness. Therefore, you cannot add good to yourself, but through persistent practice you can learn to let good flow out from within your own being.
- Joel S. Goldsmith

Perhaps the greatest human secret is the fact that every one of you was born "batteries included" ready to go! Therefore, for much of your lives you are in search for what you think you do not have or what was somehow missing from your package. This is a fruitless, frustrating and depressing journey to nowhere. Continually thinking, thinking, thinking and scheming in various ways (though few admit this) to GET, GET, GET some "need" met has made a world of insanity and chaos.

Right here, right now is everything you need, inside of YOU. As you are perhaps waiting for someone to fulfill your imagined needs, you are sitting on a goldmine waiting to be mined and made good use of. And it begins with AWARENESS. Your body knows just how to heal itself and to bring itself back into balance without effort or struggle. Your Consciousness knows how to align with all the resources you could ever need to live a happy, peaceful, prosperous and successful life. Be aware of this - that is step one and the most important step. What good is a gold mine if you don't know you own it?

You are a Center of Divine Consciousness - a Center of Divine Activity and Flow, yet you forget this quite frequently and go scrambling and worrying about things that would be easily taken care of if you would simply get in alignment with the Truth of Who you are. Within you is every answer, every resource, every solution to every problem, waiting to be turned to. Turn within now. Quiet your mind, slow down, relax your shoulders and take 3 deep breaths as you focus on opening up. But instead of thinking of opening up to receive - this time open up and IMAGINE that you are CIRCULATING Divine Light by first pouring it out from your heart space into the world around you, and then see it coming back into your heart space in a huge circular stream - much like the blood pumps out of your heart, through the veins and then back to the heart again. See it all STARTING WITH AND FROM YOU. You are the one who initiates everything in your life. Call off the search.

<u>Money Magic Mantra</u>:

I am joyously pouring out positive energy which comes back to me blessed and multiplied!

DAY 24: I'VE DECIDED TO PROSPER!

The power of decision is my own.
- A Course in Miracles

We are well into the program now and want to make sure that you are understanding more fully that there is no place for idle passive wishing and hoping if you are ever going to awaken from victim consciousness and recognize yourself as the CREATOR of your every experience. And this means becoming very comfortable and adept at making CONSCIOUS decisions every day, all day long.

EVERYONE is making decisions every day, all day long - it's just that most have NO IDEA that is what they are doing. They are deciding unconsciously by default through old mental habit patterns. These are frequently mental habit patterns of lack, limitation and scarcity. Ick!

But YOU have at least made some decision that YOU want to awaken to your Divine Nature as the creator of your life rather than as the passive observer of "the serial adventures of the body." THEREFORE, We want to know if you are awake enough, and comfortable enough with the idea of prosperity, success, money, joy, and thriving to actually DECIDE for them rather than wishing and hoping for them? Have you given up your loyalty to suffering, struggling and playing weak and helpless?

Money Magic Mantra:

I have DECIDED to prosper and thrive TODAY!

DAY 25: I RELEASE AND LET GO.

The correction of fear is your responsibility. When you ask
for release from fear, you are implying that it is not . . . You
are much too tolerant of mind wandering, and are passively
condoning your mind's miscreations.
- A Course in Miracles

Financial fear is perhaps the most dominant fear on your
planet, and this is mostly because you equate money with
survival. This is clearly a very low vibrational frequency of
thought and one that must be transformed if you are to thrive
and live as joyously as you were meant to! In other words,
you must STOP terrifying yourself! You are the one who is
doing it you know. "The calls are coming from inside the
house."

Instead, you should be continually soothing yourself into
alignment with the Higher Frequencies by turning away
from the media whose sole purpose is to frighten you into
doing whatever it is they want you to do on that particular
day. YOU HAVE CONSULTED A HIGHER
AUTHORITY, remember? The world economy is NOT your
source and never has been. CONSCIOUSNESS IS YOUR
LOVING SOURCE.

So, let go, let go, let go. Let go of schemes and plans to.
protect and defend against loss. Let go of survival strategies.
Let go of trying to manipulate and control yourself with fear.
Remember that you are literally made of Stardust and are a
LUMINOUS vessel of Divine Light walking the Earth for a
while to SHINE, SHINE, SHINE. Therefore, there is nothing

to fear. Release fear and worry as you remember that LIFE LOVES YOU and love pursues you. Be still and KNOW.

Money Magic Mantra:

There is nothing to fear. I release and let go of all financial fears and worries as I remember that I am royalty in the Kingdom and there is nothing I cannot be, or do, or have!

DAY 26: I'VE SET MY MIND ON FEELING JOY.

This brings me to the most important thing I want to say; namely, that if you want to change your life, if you want to be healthier, happier, younger, more prosperous; and above all, if you want to get nearer to God and I know that you *do* - you must change your thought and keep it changed. That is the secret of controlling your life, and there is no other way. Jesus Himself could not have done it any other way because this is a cosmic law.
Change your thought and keep it changed.
- Emmet Fox

Brother Emmet could not be more correct in his powerful charge that you must not vacillate constantly between fear and faith. You've got to set your mind on the good and KEEP IT SET NO MATTER WHAT. "Judge not according to (limiting) appearances" is still true today.

We want to remind you that nothing is more ATTRACTIVE and MAGNETIC to ALL forms of good than a JOYFUL person! We are not talking about pasting a phony smile on your face to cover your rage and depression. We mean GENUINE JOY that comes from FOCUSING like a laser on any positive aspect that you can find in your now moment - even if it is remembering a joyous moment from the past or imagining a happy one to come.

This joy may not even show on your face to others. It is not a performance. It is an inner experience of peaceful, relaxed calm delight and gentle receptivity. It is the opposite of chewing endlessly on your plans to solve your problems, shape up other people, or fix fix fix this, that or the other thing. Instead, you decide to chew on every single thing that is RIGHT in your world and in YOU and in anyone who crosses your mind.

True prosperity LOVES joyous grateful people.

<u>Money Magic Mantra</u>:

I am a joyous prosperous being and wonderful things fall in my lap all the time

DAY 27: I HAVE AN EXPANDING WEALTH CONSCIOUSNESS.

Nor can you get anywhere by affirming that all that the Father has belongs to you. That is true in theory, but in practice only your consciousness of specific money determines what you shall get . . . Make your affirmative treatment, "I have the consciousness of x dollars a week." Demonstrate that amount. Then, give yourself another raise as you grow in consciousness.
- Dr. Robert Bitzer

Practice being definite in your prosperity. To be definite is the opposite of being indecisive and wishy-washy. Again, dissolve wishing and hoping as you SET YOUR MIND and KEEP IT SET, without knowing HOW this prosperity (or any other manifestation) will happen. The Infinite Intelligence knows the ways and means you know not of and will move you along if you remain soft, open, relaxed and CONFIDENT in the Principle you are using.

The idea of "more money" is too vague and wishy-washy. One "extra" dollar a week is "more money." Start to stretch yourself by stating how much more you are willing to manifest.

That's all. Work with that for now. Fill in the amount below and then affirm it frequently for the rest of the 90 days.

Money Magic Mantra:

I have the consciousness of _____ dollars per week (or month or year).

DAY 28: I SEE AND FEEL MYSELF AS A PROSPEROUS, HAPPY AND SUCCESSFUL BEING.

Everything can be taken from us but one thing; the last of the human freedoms - to choose one's attitude in any given set of circumstances, to choose one's own way.
- Viktor Frankl

You might be very surprised to find out how many multi-millionaires feel very fearful when it comes to money - or how many professional models feel unattractive and undesirable - or how many famous award winners feel unworthy and like a phony - and how many people who have achieved tremendous things feel like losers.

You see, it's not about what happens "out there" but is 100% an inside job. So, in the end, it's not really the "thing" or even the experiences in life you are really seeking but rather the FEELING you think those things would bring you. And the cosmic joke of it is that for the most part, you could feel that RIGHT NOW without anything changing at all. No one can make you feel anything about yourself or your life except YOU! YOU SET THE BAR for yourself. You rule your own mind, mouth, moods and attitudes. Others may have had extreme influence over you, but ultimately YOU are in control of yourself.

Choose your feeling and your thoughts. Yes, CHOOSE them. You CAN. It takes practice, but it is the greatest activity there is in terms of the fruit that it will bear. Get off the treadmill of trying to GET SOMEWHERE and start to see and feel the way you want to right now. It's all happening in YOUR head anyhow. There is no such thing as later. There is only the eternal now. SEE AND FEEL IT NOW in your imagination (which is where you are really living anyhow). Then, watch how everything around you starts to reflect the inner - and usually very quickly.

<u>Money Magic Mantra</u>:

I SEE and FEEL myself as prosperous, happy and successful in life! The evidence keeps mounting!

DAY 29: I AM LEARNING TO ENJOY THE PROCESS OF PROSPEROUS THINKING AND LIVING.

Only infinite patience produces immediate results.
- A Course in Miracles

HOW is not your part - you are probably familiar with that by now. But We also want to tell you that WHEN is not your part either! LET GO, LET GO, LET GO. Let go of time because you only make it take LONGER if you are like the kid in the back seat endlessly saying, "Are we there yet, are we there yet, are we there yet?"

Impatience doubles the time you'll have to wait - because it is HUGE RESISTANCE. If it were up to humans, you'd try to create a baby in a weekend instead of over a 9-month period. If you want to go faster, slow down. Don't forget, this is "Opposite World", and it is 180 degrees away from the ways you were taught by the human world. The truth is, the more relaxed and patient you are, the more smoothly and quickly it will all seem to happen.

So, you can still be definite about what you want, but let go of the timing and ways and form. Go more for the FEELING. Calm way way down and stop taking score so much. Only take score of what there is to appreciate and praise each day. Take score of the gifts of each moment. And as much as possible remind yourself you are always at the right place at the right time and that all things are unfolding in perfect Divine Order as long as you stay centered in Truth. Fear not. Be not afraid. Take your time. All is truly well.

Money Magic Mantra:

I am learning to enjoy and trust the process of prospering thinking and living. There is no need to worry or rush. The Universe has perfect timing.

DAY 30: DIVINE LOVE IS MY PROSPERING POWER.

Miracles occur naturally as expressions of love.
The real miracle is the love that inspires them.
In this sense everything that comes from love is a miracle.
- A Course in Miracles

Most humans put money at one end of a stick and love on the extreme other end. They believe that love and money have absolutely nothing to do with each other - and many think that love and money are in opposition and at war somehow. This is complete nonsense, for some of the wealthiest humans on your planet got that way by doing things they LOVE to do! Once again, Opposite World! You've been taught the exact opposite of Spiritual Truth and find yourself frustrated and upset when it creates such struggle and suffering.

A "miracle" is nothing more or less than the shift from human fear consciousness to a consciousness of Divine Love. Divine Love is impersonal non-attached love. It is not cheap sentimentality nor is it even affection necessarily. It is IN you but not OF you. It is there because you are an extension of Divine Love Itself, which is another word for God or Source or First Cause or Divine Mind. A rose by any other name or a God by any other name. Same, same, same.

Therefore, We are urging you to DECLARE and INVOKE Divine Love in ALL areas of your life - particularly in terms of your work and money where you are most likely to leave love out of the picture. IMAGINE everyone and everything that has anything to do with your work and money being

INFUSED with IMPERSONAL Divine Love. See everyone happy, thriving and joyously cooperating for the highest good of all. Release and bless everyone as you remember that it is love that gives everything meaning. Know that YOU are a CIRCULATOR of Divine Love and that your work is not a job, but a ministry. You are there to circulate Divine Love! There is nothing that it cannot accomplish if you will commit yourself to invoking It in ALL of your affairs and undertakings!

Money Magic Mantra:

Impersonal Divine Love now guides, prospers, inspires and makes joyful use of me! Divine Love is my prospering power and my only success strategy!

DAY 31: PROSPERITY IS NATURAL FOR ME.

Of course, the idea that hard work and struggle are inevitable is nonsense. Inside the energy of abundance, there is no struggle, only flow. If you are struggling, there is something about your thinking or your modus that needs adjustment. Effort is a natural part of our physical state, but struggle is effort laced with emotion, and that is unnatural and unholy.
You don't need it.
- Stuart Wilde

Perhaps you thought that lessons on prosperity would be filled with cutting edge strategies on what to DO, DO, DO to GET MONEY into your life! Ahhhh, did you forget about Opposite World again? The Spiritual Truth is that prosperity is perfectly natural. It is poverty that is unnatural. It is a kind of mental illness which needs to be neutralized, dissolved and sent back to the nothingness so that peace and sanity can be restored.

YOUR PART is to LET GO of strategies and the obsession with DOING so that you can RELAX INTO THE FLOW of the River of Life More ABUNDANT! If something is not working, not flowing, the answer isn't to PUSH AND TRY HARDER AND HARDER AND HARDER. STOP. Take a few steps back. Become very still inside. Let go of judging the situation and giving it so much meaning and importance. STOP trying to fix, manage and figure it all out. BREATHE. Release all struggle and strain.

Get in touch with the Forces beyond the appearances. Let go of what other say or think, of what the world is doing, of what you see others doing. Let all that shit go and turn within yourself to your CONNECTION to Infinite Wisdom. Listen. Feel. Sense. And if that does not come easily right now - GO PLAY! Dance. Sing. Take a walk or a nap. Watch a funny movie. Throw the ball for the dog. Pet the cat. Masturbate. Bake a cake. Tinker with the motor of the car. DISTRACT YOURSELF in a happy way and then come back to the situation with a fresh OPEN mind. You will be much more IN THE FLOW of prosperity and INSPIRATION rather than pressured motivation.

All is well with you. You may just not have realized it yet.

Money Magic Mantra:

I don't have to have all the answers. While I rest and play my Spirit is guiding me back into alignment with the Flow of prosperous good!

DAY 32: THINGS ARE ALWAYS MAGICALLY WORKING OUT FOR ME!

What could you not accept, if you but knew that everything that happens, all events, past present and to come, are gently planned by One Whose only purpose is your good?
- A Course in Miracles

Please do not misunderstand this lesson. The One Whose only purpose is your good is not some dude in the sky on a throne, pulling strings on your life as if you were a puppet. There is nothing outside of you. The Divine Presence is WITHIN YOU, not "up there" somewhere. And nothing is more delicious than the relationship between you and your Inner Source when you accept it as real.

This Divine Inner Presence is working WITH you and knows ways and means that you are not consciously aware of. It is RESPONDING to YOU and it goes about planning whatever it is that you're focusing on. It does not make judgments between "good and bad" in the least. It assumes that you know what you are doing and so It assumes it is all "good." If you focus on poverty and sacrifice and struggle, It plans those experiences out as if they were your greatest good. It's like magic. You think and it begins to act on the thought. It does not decide for you or judge what you are giving your attention to at all.

Once you can accept that this is the way of things, you can let go of confusion and being wishy-washy about what you allow into your mind and consciousness. You will take responsibility for your own life, your happiness and what you get out of each day and every experience. This is the beginning of living as a deliberate creator rather than as a passive observer who is creating by default. You will begin to see that it's all "magically" working out according to your own energy, consciousness and vibration (which are all the same thing actually).

So, DECIDE now and each day what you will focus on. Guard your mind, mouth, moods and attitudes so that things will magically work out in ways that feel good to YOU rather than them magically going straight to hell. Remember, if you don't like how you feel, it is because of something you are thinking or the way you are focusing your attention and energy. And a thought can always be changed.

Money Magic Mantra:

As I take responsibility for thinking of what brings me joy,
my life unfolds in the most delightful ways!

DAY 33: I AM SAFE.

Money is not evil. It is nothing. But no one here can live without illusions, for she must yet strive to have the last illusion be accepted by everyone everywhere. She has a mighty part in this one purpose, for which she came. She stays here but for this. And while she stays she will be given what she needs to stay.
- A Course in Miracles Psychotherapy: Purpose, Process and Practice

---

We want to tell you, or remind you, that Earth is a temp assignment, not a permanent gig. No one is staying - no one. Therefore, there is nothing "here" that you can ever truly own or that is yours. EVERYTHING is temporarily yours to use - as it would be if you worked for a temp agency and were sent to an office to work for two weeks. The company would supply all your needs - computer, desk, phone, paper clips, break room, vending machines, etc. Whatever is necessary for you to comfortably get the job done is there for you to use.

And since it is a temp job, you don't get all caught up in the CHEAP DRAMA of "titles," business cards, prestige, ambition, inter-office politics and gossip. You show up, prepared, on time, doing what you agreed to do, with a good attitude. All the rest is none of your business and out of your control. Well, that IS what the Earth Assignment is like too if you would only realize it.

So, RELAX. ENJOY your time here. Fear not. Be not afraid. You are on a need-to-know basis and all that you need is yours to requisition from Head Office. Your REAL job is JOYOUS EXPANSION as part of the "Mystic Protection Program." Everything else is just a cover. Whatever you want or need will be provided in perfect timing and ways for you to do what you came here to do - joyously expand so that others may see your Light which glorifies the Source which you are a part of. Loosen up baby! It's the best gig in the Cosmos!

Money Magic Mantra:

I always have whatever I want and need to joyously expand. How is not my part.

DAY 34: I BELIEVE IN MY SUCCESS.

Know that nothing can hinder you but yourself. If you
believe that you can, you can. If you believe that the Law of
Good will work, It will work.
- Ernest Holmes, The Art of Life

Belief is not "psyching yourself up" to PUSH through to
some perceived good. It is CULTIVATED like a garden or a
farm. Even though We like to use the word "magic" it really
is much more of a natural science which is not understood by
the masses. You plant a seed of belief and take care of it by
watering it with love and faith, weeding out the fear and
negativity, and not digging it up every day to see if the roots
are growing. You TRUST the process and you believe it is
working even before you see the first shoots coming up
through the earth.

Cultivating prosperity is really not much different than
cultivating a flower garden or a farm of crops. It's takes
patience, care, understanding and daily attention. And there
is no comparison. It is not "better" to have a huge farm or
greenhouse than it is to have a flower box in a window and a
tomato plant growing on the kitchen counter. This is a highly
individualized curriculum and not a "one size fits all"
philosophy. Some people like to be very very busy and
others like lots of time for rest. Let go of looking over the
fence at your neighbor's yard or garden. DO YOU. Judge
not according to appearances. Go by your FEELINGS of
good within!

Believe in YOUR success - by YOUR standards. Don't sell yourself short with lack of confidence and don't go big just to impress people who really don't give a shit what you're doing anyhow. Find your own sweet spot in prosperity and know that if you believe you can, you can. No rush. No worry. Don't try to rush the growing season. All is well.

Money Magic Mantra:

I am cultivating a garden of prosperous good and I love watching it grow!

DAY 35: I FORGIVE MY PAST MONEY MISTAKES.

Our forgiving "all people" includes ourselves. You must also forgive yourself. Let the finger of denial erase every sin or "falling short" that you have charged up against yourself. Pay your debt by saying to that part of yourself which you think has fallen short: "Thou are made whole . . . "
- Charles Fillmore, Prosperity

Most humans are taught about money by default and through trial and error, which is a terrible way to learn. You observe how those close to you talk about, handle and use money but very rarely are any of you sat down and given clear, sane, helpful instructions about money and finances. So it is no wonder so many struggle with the entire concept! There is so much shame and guilt surrounding something that is nothing more than an exchange of energy.

And it is nearly impossible to live a human lifetime without making mistakes in the use or even misuse of money. BIG DEAL! SO WHAT? It's TIME to release the guilt, blame, shame, fear and regrets around money! We want you to make a list of your self-judgments around your money past or even present if it is still happening. Write it all out - you spent too much, "wasted" it, are greedy, use it to buy love or to control others, trusted the wrong people, hoarded it or squandered it, felt unworthy to have it, sold out on yourself to get some, felt superior for having it, lied about it, hid it, and on and on. Leave nothing out.

THEN, give it all to the God of your understanding - to the Loving Divine Source within. Apologize to yourself and then let that shit go! Shred or burn the list and start fresh right here, right now. Ask Spirit to continue to teach you the ways of money wisdom and know that as you ask, it is given. And the Universe is ready to start over fresh and new in every instant, so there is no need for punishment or long delays in turning your relationship with money from negative to very positive! Light removes darkness at the speed of light.

Money Magic Mantra:

I forgive myself for any mistakes I've made around money and I am now learning the wise joyous peaceful use of money in my life. I trust myself and I trust my Source to guide me.

DAY 36: I LOOK FOR THE POSITIVE ASPECTS IN EVERYTHING.

Treat a man as he is, and he will remain as he is.
Treat a man as he could be,
and he will become what he should be.
- Ralph Waldo Emerson

As a Deliberate Creator, you need to be AWARE of how your energy, focus and attention are contributing to whatever is happening in your proverbial yard. Creation is not simply a result of what you are focusing on but rather the ENERGY and CONSCIOUSNESS you are activating within YOURSELF AS YOU FOCUS ON whatever it is. You can focus on prosperity and be activating energy of despair, bondage, limitation and anger, OR you can be activating energies of JOY, peace, limitlessness and freedom!

Your world is not happening to you - it is RESPONDING to your ENERGY! Therefore, if something is frustrating you or seems stuck or is a problem, you either need to walk away from it entirely, turn your attention from it entirely OR start changing YOUR ENERGY by making lists of the positive aspects of whatever it is. You do not make positive change in anything by resisting, judging, attacking or giving "constructive" criticism. You make positive change by CHANGING YOUR MIND and beating the drum of gratitude and appreciation - even if you start out very begrudgingly. In fact, gratitude, appreciation and making lists of positive aspects are the most powerful tools you have in creating a lift that is nothing short of MAGICAL!

If ANYTHING or ANYONE is bothering you today, stop playing "ain't it awful!?" and get busy doing lists of positive aspects until you FEEL your energy shift. Then, watch the magic happen.

Money Magic Mantra:

I create daily magic by making lists of the positive aspects of everything I see in my world!

DAY 37: THERE IS NO LIMIT ON MY PROSPERITY POTENTIAL.

If you say you are on a fixed income,
my question is, "who fixed it?"
- Terry Cole-Whittaker

Everything in your experience is a result of how you are flowing your energy. Do not forget, it is done unto you as you BELIEVE - and it is done BY YOU! It's all a matter of consciousness, consciousness, consciousness. If YOU say your income is fixed and limited - so be it. If you say that your income is constantly expanding - so be it.

You might want to say, "I've decided that I'm not going to participate in the recession, depression, or downward economic trends," and if you mean it then you have kept your valves open and the great Mother Tao will flow prosperity to you regardless of what anyone else is being, doing or having. You pension, trust fund, salary, and so on are NOT your source unless YOU say so. And then you have every reason to be very afraid for none of these things can be counted on.

But if you see Divine Mind as the Source of your good then you are limitless indeed. There is no "glass ceiling" to even break through. You are not living "outside the box" but have come to see that the box is just a story that was made up by victim consciousness to keep the status quo going. That has NOTHING to do with you, you glorious sexy fabulous Deliberate Creator! We will keep reminding you of this because We know how loud the physical world can get with all the Chicken Little's running around screeching.

Money Magic Mantra:

My limitless income is constantly expanding in wonderful
unexpected ways!

DAY 38: IT'S ONLY NATURAL THAT
I BECOME RICHER AND RICHER.

Please note that the word "rich" means having an abundance
of good or living a fuller, more satisfying life. Indeed, you
are prosperous to the degree that you are experiencing peace,
health, happiness and plenty in your world.
- Catherine Ponder

Well-being is lined up outside your door because abundance
is the NATURAL Law of the Universe. Remember, nature is
lavish and extravagant, not miserly and limited. Therefore,
prosperity and riches are more natural than poverty and lack.
You have only to OPEN the portals of your Consciousness
to let in all the good. OPEN TO RECEIVE instead of
struggling to get or keep.

Let go of what others are thinking or doing. Let go of trying
to get the approval of a world of miserable people and
instead join up with the Great Cosmic Conspiracy! It is a
Conspiracy to bless, prosper and uplift you! Everything is set
up for you to succeed in life without endless sacrifice and
suffering. But YOU have to take the bold courageous step of
being completely disloyal to any old programming which
glorifies poverty and suffering as being holy, spiritual or the
will of some dude up in the sky.

By the way, there are NO TESTS given to anyone, ever.
That is simply another religious myth. Everything comes
because it is a vibrational match to the thinker. Release the
belief that you are ever being tested or that there is
something "spiritually" wrong with wanting to get more

good out of life. It's why you came here in the first place - to create and experience the JOY of being a CREATOR! So, get with the program and relax your way into alignment with the Divine Conspiracy of making YOU richer and richer!

Money Magic Mantra:

I give myself permission to get richer and richer in the most joyous and effortless ways.

DAY 39: I AM EASY TO CONTRIBUTE TO.

Nothing can flow through a closed valve.
Make it easy for people to contribute to you.
- Jacob

Jacob tells a story of a homeless woman in Los Angeles who approached him for money one sunny Saturday afternoon on the streets of West Hollywood. She was particularly dirty and was half-naked as her oversized t shirt was torn and hanging so low her breast was almost completely exposed. Jacob said that he had no cash on him and without missing a beat she replied, "Do you have Venmo?" SHE WAS MAKING IT EASY TO CONTRIBUTE TO HER! She was READY and OPEN! Jacob didn't even have the Venmo app yet (which is for sending money electronically) but this woman did and was ready to accept money.

Many people want help, will even say they desperately NEED help, and yet they make it a pain in the ass to actually help them. They've made it difficult to contribute to them! They don't know it, but they are closing off the valves through which the Cosmic Energy can flow. Hinting and whining are not signs that your valves are open to receive. DECLARING exactly what you want and then PREPARING for it to show up - THAT is the power that opens your valves to let the good in!

If you ask someone to help you move, make sure when they arrive with the truck that you have packed all the boxes and are ready to load and go. If you ask someone to take you to the airport, be packed and have your bags by the door

BEFORE they arrive at your home. Don't ask and then make the giver wait for you to get your act together.

PREPARE FOR THE DEMONSTRATION YOU WANT BEFORE IT COMES.

<u>Money Magic Mantra</u>:

I prepare for my prosperity demonstration and am making it easy for Source to give me what I want! I am ready!

DAY 40: I TRUST MY SOURCE.

When a person is calm, complex events appear simple. To know what is happening, push less, open out and be aware. See without staring. Listen quietly rather than listening hard. Use intuition and reflection rather than trying to figure things out. The more you can let go of trying, and the more open and receptive you become, the more easily you will know what is happening.
- John Heider, The Tao of Leadership

Brother Jesus told the people to consider the lilies of the field and the birds of the air. They do not worry or spin themselves into a frenzy and yet they are gloriously provided for by the Source. And you are certainly as important to the Source as any bird of flower.

So please, be still - even for a moment. Just stop. Relax your shoulders and unclench your jaw. Slow down to the speed of Grace. Let go of strategies and attempts to manipulate, fix, control, clutch or grab. BREATHE. It's all okay. Not going to be okay, IS okay. Well Being abounds and is natural. You were meant to thrive WITHOUT struggle and suffering. Stop auditioning and "selling" yourself. Simply show up as YOU. That is enough. That was the Plan all along. You don't need to add anything to it.

Place your future in the Hands of Source and TRUST the process - trust the Source. All is well whether you can presently see that or not. If you can do this, you will soon not only trust the process, but you can also begin to ENJOY the process of watching how cleverly Source works things out without your endless worrying and silly interventions and "helping."

Money Magic Mantra:

I trust the Source within me to work everything out today and always as I mentally relax and release all worry and fear. Everything is always working out for me in effortless ways.

DAY 41: MY RELATIONSHIPS ARE ABUNDANTLY LOVING, HARMONIOUS AND JOYFUL!

Divine love expressing through me now draws to me all that is needed to make me happy and to make my life complete.
- Catherine Ponder

The concept lonely rich person is not only a cliche but is also is not really possible because if you are lonely, you are not truly rich. You may have billions of dollars in the bank and own half the world, but you are quite poor if you do not have joyous personal relationships. This is also quite easy to turn around. It is nothing more than a negative mental habit pattern - some silly belief that is being repeated with monotonous regularity.

Begin by knowing and affirming that you are a wonderful person and that it is possible to attract other wonderful people who will be a match to you. Declare that you bring out the best in each other and that all your relationships are mutually loving and beneficial. Let go of any labels you have put on yourself such as: lonely, shy, timid, too weird, sickly, too sensitive, empath, introvert and so on. These are just ways of separating yourself from others and mean nothing. They were made up by "experts" and mean NOTHING. YOU are a GOD BEING and if you must have a label, this one will do nicely. Therefore, you are unlimited, and all things are possible for you.

And since all minds are joined in the One Mind, spend some time each day quieting your mind as you mentally and emotionally send out a psychic invitation to those who would be the ideal companions to come into your life. Do not think of specific people but only of the qualities you would most enjoy in friends and companions. Then, let it go and go on with your day. Soon enough you will notice that you are becoming magnetic, and you will be rich in loving supportive and happy relationships.

<u>Money Magic Mantra</u>:

I am rich in wonderful relationships with wonderful people. My life is full and fabulous.

DAY 42: THERE ARE NO LIMITS ON MY FINANCIAL INCOME.

I have a wonderful job, in a wonderful way.
I give wonderful service, for wonderful pay!
- Florence Scovel Shinn

Actor Peter Boyle was 61 when he was hired for the TV show "Everybody Loves Raymond." And he credited the above affirmative statement to his landing the job! He said that he got it from Catherine Ponder's book "Pray and Grow Rich" and that he used the power of visualization. He was an "actor for hire" as most are in that industry, so it is quite easy to feel at the effect of other people and things outside of himself as most humans do. Instead, he DECIDED that HE was the captain of his own fate.

In fact, he arrived at the audition very irritated and NOT in the good friendly mood you might think you would need in order to get "people in power" to "like" and want you. He'd gotten lost on the way there, been given wrong information, and was very cranky with the people who had the power to give him the job. It just so happened that cranky was the major personality trait of the character he was auditioning to play. There are no accidents. You have no idea HOW Source will line things up when YOU line up with the Universal Flow of Well Being.

YOUR PART is to visualize, affirm and accept the best and then just be yourself. And though Jacob always likes to remind everyone to show up with a good attitude, even a bad attitude can be used and helpful IF your MAIN attitude is one of positive BELIEF and alignment with your greater good!

Money Magic Mantra:

The power to create my good is not out there in the world. The power is in me!

DAY 43: I LET GO OF STRUGGLE
AND RELAX INTO WELL-BEING.

What is it that you are practicing on an ongoing basis that
you are keeping active in your vibration? Because whatever
it is, eventually becomes not only an active vibration, but it
also becomes a dominant vibration on those subjects. And
whatever is the dominant vibration within you (whatever
you've practiced the most) becomes your point of attraction.
- Esther Hicks (Abraham)

There is never anything to fear. Truly. Never. All is truly
well for there are no limits to the good that you can be, do
and have. There is simply no need to push against the flow
of Life by swimming upstream. ALL your good is
DOWNstream! We want you to begin to EXPECT things to
go well for you. We want to you expect joyous expansion
rather than decline and contraction. We want you to trust
your Source rather than trusting your ability to "figure shit
out."

What this is about is ending the war - the mental war within.
There is a tendency among many humans to immediately
trust bad news and to be very suspicious about
WONDERFUL news! How ridiculous. You are living in a
FRIENDLY Universe that is loving you more than you could
ever imagine. But YOU must PRACTICE the vibration of
trust rather than the vibration of worry.

Many of you may have been reprimanded by an adult at
some point to get your head out of the clouds and stop your
foolish daydreaming. Well, worry is mentally imagining and

PRETENDING that everything is falling apart. Day dreaming is mentally imagining and PRETENDING that everything is falling together. Which sounds more fun to you?

<u>Money Magic Mantra</u>:

Everything in my life keeps falling together, keeps falling together, keeps falling together.

DAY 44: I WILL NOT ARGUE
FOR MY PERCEIVED LIMITATIONS.

Argue for your limitations and sure enough, they're yours.
- Richard Bach

As much as humans say they want freedom or joyous expansion it is staggering the degree to which they stubbornly cling to being right and to defending whatever limiting beliefs they've taken on. In fact, the person who thinks of themselves as a real progressive type these days is exactly the one who is also most likely to become extremely angry when their limiting beliefs are challenged. Dear soul, do not be one of those pitiful creatures.

You live in a culture filled with those who continually "cut off their nose to spite their face" on a regular basis - and often thinking they are the clever ones. Very clever people without a nose. They will "not give this or that person or institution the satisfaction of blah, blah, blah." Oh dear. Spitting into the wind and thinking they've shown the wind.

If you want to truly prosper, let all that nonsense go. No one is trying to "get you." That's YOU. The world is neutral. It only reflects you back to you. There is nothing to fear. Nothing to argue against. Nothing to defend against. Nothing. You are safe. If someone steals everything you have, including your identity, they've taken nothing at all. If you stay connected to Source you can have that and more back and better than what you lost. We know where everything is and how to make more and make it better. Forget your so-called limitations and trust the Source. Stop talking yourself down. Stop depreciating yourself with ridiculous "casual conversation." There is no such thing as casual conversation. ALL conversation is CAUSAL because it CREATES YOUR reality.

<u>Money Magic Mantra</u>:

I am a worthy, gorgeous, prosperous,
brilliant limitless being of LIGHT!

DAY 45: "THANK YOU" SEALS THE DEAL OF MY PROSPERITY.

I went to give the man a dollar tip and as I looked down at our hands, I saw it was actually five dollars. We both saw it at the same time and the man said, "Thank you Reverend Ike" - and we all know that "thank you" seals the deal. Always give thanks first to bring the manifestation.

- Reverend Ike

The way to hasten your good is to live in a state of constant gratitude and thanksgiving for your all your present good, and your future good even though it is not yet evident in the physical. Gratitude sets your Consciousness into having instead of wanting what is lacking. In this sense, it is part of the Law of Assumption - and an assumption if persisted in, will harden into fact.

Let your gratitude and praise be constant, but keep in mind it is not to some mythical dude in the sky. You are thanking GOD-IN-YOU for handling it all with joyous ease for you.

- Thank You Source for resolving my relationship issue.

- Thank You Source for calming my mind and opening my heart.

- Thank You Source for helping me let go of that grievance.

- Thank You Source for healing my body and restoring my health.

- Thank You Source for providing the ideal gig.

- Thank You Source for guiding my daughter.

And on and on like that all day long. It is a state of awareness that IN YOU is the Divine Answer to every challenge that ever faces you, as well as the limitless resources and guidance to prosper you in every area of your life.

<u>Money Magic Mantra</u>:

When I give thanks I am sealing the deal of my ever-expanding prosperous good - even BEFORE it arrives!

DAY 46: I AM ONE WITH THE LIMITLESS SOURCE OF ALL GOOD!

You do not have to compel God to give you good things,
any more than you have to use your will power
to make the sun rise.
- Wallace D. Wattles

It is as natural for you to prosper as it is for the sun to rise each morning. Poverty and lack are actually unnatural and are learned mental attitudes. These mental habit patterns of lack and fear can be undone by replacing them with Spiritual Truth and Light.

The Universe is forever giving, giving, giving forth from limitless bountiful good. There is no hoarding in the Universe and there is no withholding. Therefore, be like the natural Universe and pour forth if you want to receive. Be what Jacob calls a "go-allower" rather than a "go-getter." As you pour forth whatever good you have, you cast your bread upon the waters and they must return to you. This is not a matter of sacrifice nor of hard work but of the courage to move past fear and resistance in order to live more FREELY and joyously. After all, you do nothing each day to deserve the sun rising up or the song of the birds or the oxygen you breathe.

When you know yourself as ONE with all of Creation, you also know that there is never anything missing. Everything is provided if you can align yourself with Eternal Truth and RELAX into the CIRCULATION of Energy. You must breathe out in order to make space to breathe in. You must give love if you want to be in a position to receive love. You must let go of a "get" mentality and get into a mentality of endless joyous circulation. Be a "go-allower" or a "go-circulator" of positive energy and watch what happens! If you are in a place of lack, POUR FORTH from what you have in order to prime the pump. Planting a seed comes BEFORE there is a reaping of the harvest. Give to abundance, not to poverty and "neediness" in your tithes for you will reap what you sow to. Tithe to where you are spiritually fed, and give your "alms" to the poor secretly with no fanfare and telling no one.

Money Magic Mantra:

I am a joyous GO-ALLOWER because it is so fun to circulate energy and watch it come back to me in the most delightful effortless ways!

DAY 47: NOTHING IS TOO GOOD TO BE TRUE FOR ME!

Guilt is a sure sign that your thinking is unnatural.
- A Course in Miracles

No peacock feels embarrassed about having such gorgeous plumage. The dogs and cats living in the White House or in Royal Palaces across the world do not wonder if they deserve to live in such lavish surroundings. No baby feels awkward being given such constant attention and praise! But many of you have trained yourselves to think that the good things in life need to come only after long hard struggling and that they need to be JUSTIFIED to the world, or that they are only for the lucky few. There are many more ridiculous unnatural ways you've been taught to think, but all you need to know is that that it is all utter nonsense. Let it go and wake up to joyous expansive living NOW.

We want to remind you that prosperity, health, love, joy, inner peace, wonderful work, harmonious happy relationships, fun, play, creativity and so much more are THE NATURAL ORDER of things. They are not the result of "miracles" or even of "magic" but are the fruits of a Consciousness that is turned toward them. Yes, there are seasons of things in the physical and the tides do go in and go out so you will certainly have contrast between wanted and unwanted. But that contrast does not have to be the extremes of feast or famine, typhoons or droughts.

Yes, money goes up and down, some relationships will come into your life and others may go, health can be out of balance for a bit before returning to equanimity again. But these can be GENTLE rather than dramatic shifts if you will learn to live in the state We like to call "calm delight." There is never any reason to feel guilty or embarrassed about any wonderful thing in your life. Nor is there any reason to panic when challenges and problems arise. No guilt, no shame, no blame. Stay centered in calm delight, which is a state of being inwardly relaxed and outwardly grateful and appreciative. It is also a state of EXPECTING the good rather than expecting problems. Gratitude always primes the pump and if you can be JOYOUSLY grateful even in the presence of challenges, you are truly a Master of Manifestation and your problems will not be able to cling to you for very long, if at all.

So, We want you to begin to notice if you ever feel guilty or fearful about your good and then let those thoughts go by affirming that nothing is too good for you, nothing too good to be true. Your good is never a fluke, a miracle or anything other than the result of right thinking and right feeling.

Money Magic Mantra:

I watch in calm delight as my greater good unfolds before me in wonderful easy peasy ways.

DAY 48: I SEE BEYOND LIMITING APPEARANCES TO THE PROSPEROUS TRUTH!

There is no labor from which people shrink as they do from that of sustained and consecutive thought; it is the hardest work in the world. This is especially true when truth is contrary to appearances. Every appearance in the visible world tends to produce a corresponding form in the mind which observes it; and this can only be prevented by holding the thought of the TRUTH. - Wallace D. Wattles

––––––––––––––

To change your thought to the prosperous positives and keep it changed is your work. Judging according to appearances is going to keep you recreating whatever appears before you in the moment. So, if what you are looking at is limitation and scarcity, that is all you will ever experience. Unless you change your mind and keep it changed. Current appearances are like reading an old newspaper - they bear witness to past thinking. NEW thoughts bring NEW appearances, if you will persist.

New tactics, new strategies, new ways of doing things will not have a fraction of the effect of a NEW way of THINKING. Consciousness is everything. Consciousness is King. Consciousness is Queen. Consciousness is what CREATES.

Whatever it is your deep desire to be or do or have or experience, it will not manifest unless you have a thought and belief that matches it BEFORE you ever see it in the physical. The thought is the seed, the physical manifestation is the plant. Very simple.

<u>Money Magic Mantra</u>:

I persistently and consistently believe in my vision long before I see the evidence.

DAY 49: IF IT'S GOING TO BE, IT'S UP TO ME.

Often good and sincere persons ask if it is right to use Divine Power for personal purposes. No one thinks it is wrong to use other laws of nature for personal purposes . . . Do not hesitate to use this law for any purpose which is constructive. It is no more selfish to use spiritual law for personal purposes than it is to plant a garden for your personal use. Moreover, there is no escaping this law, for it is as intimate as your own thought, as personal as your own being. - Ernest Holmes

---

Your life is a Garden of Consciousness. Whatever is growing in your garden is there because of thought seeds that have been sown by you, or by what you have allowed the culture and others to sow there. Life is not random, accidental or coincidental. This is a law-based Universe and there is no way to escape that Truth.

Look around your life and know that you are the one who created it - and most of it is very good indeed. You should take credit for that regardless of who "bought" or "paid" for it. If YOU are reaping the benefits in any way, it is due to YOUR planting of seeds in the soil of your subconscious and conscious mind. Be GLAD and celebrate the good you've sown and reaped - a bed to sleep in, transportation, lights in your home, people to love, clothes to wear, food to eat and on and on and on. All are there by the laws of sowing and reaping. How can it be selfish or "unspiritual" to plant what YOU want in YOUR OWN garden? No one is planting in your garden unless you are passively allowing it. There is nothing spiritual about living as a victim.

You are sowing every day, all day long. Doesn't it make sense to plant what you WANT to see grow and thrive? Greed is not wanting a big bountiful garden. Greed is wanting no one else to have any land or to have the choice to grow what THEY want. There is more than enough for everyone for the Universe is continually creating more, more, more. Volcanoes are even creating more of your very earth to walk on! The only limits are the ones YOU accept and believe.

Money Magic Mantra:

I am choosing what I want to grow in my garden by consciously sowing the right thought seeds.

DAY 50: THE MORE I GIVE, THE MORE I RECEIVE.

When you talk of hard times, famines, lack, you are talking of something that has no place in the Mind of God. You are not acknowledging God in all your ways but are acknowledging error and affirming that the world has its source in outer things. You must turn around (repent) and get into this consciousness, that in Mind, in Spirit, there is abundance. - Charles Fillmore

---

If you are preparing for leaner times, they will come to you. If your faith is in the things of the world as the source of your supply, you will find that you live in a consciousness of fear and limitation. That physical world is the extreme opposite of Truth. In fact, when you have the least is when it is the most important to give and to pour out from what you have rather than try to cling to it and thereby shut off the flow of circulation. When you stop giving, you stop receiving. Nothing could be simpler or truer.

Always give with the expectation that your good will return to you blessed, multiplied and running over! Do not give timidly and fearfully but rather filled with the joyous faith and knowledge that this is a Universe of CIRCULATION. Remember, the only two energy patterns are congestion and circulation. Nothing should be more exciting to you in terms of prosperity than your joyous giving because you know that you are always giving to yourself and are never sacrificing.

"Who understands what giving means must laugh at the idea of sacrifice." - ACIM

Money Magic Mantra:

I joyously generously give knowing that it hastens my good
and returns to me multiplied!

DAY 51: GRATITUDE HASTENS AND INCREASES MY GOOD!

The Universe loves grateful people. The more grateful you are, the more you get to be grateful about. It's that simple. - Louise L. Hay

_____

Money loves people who appreciate it. It's like everything else. Don't you appreciate the people who appreciate you more than the ones who are ambivalent about you? And don't you also avoid those who are NEEDY about your attention? It's an energy thing. A sense of calm grateful receptivity is a very attractive energy. Therefore, be grateful for the money you HAVE even if it is a very small amount. Bless it and welcome it into your life and soon enough it will bring its friends to come into your life!

You must give up the idea that money is limited or scarce or hard to get. You must give up the idea that holding onto your money with a vice-like grip will produce prosperity. You must release the idea that money has anything to do with work or your age or worldly "connections." Free money from those silly ideas and prejudices. If the very thought of money does not produce JOY in you, you have got consciousness work to do because you are caught in a nightmare that is simply not true. If you ENJOY money, money will enjoy YOU and want to be with you.

Take some time today to IMAGINE yourself playing with money and having a ball! Do not be "spiritual" about this - be JOYFUL and playful. If NO ONE would ever know what you did with the money, what would you do with 10 million dollars today?

Money Magic Mantra:

I love playing with money and money loves to play with me!

DAY 52: I FULLY EXPECT TO RECEIVE THE GOOD I DESIRE.

It is no use to desire a thing unless you expect to get it, either in part or in full. Desire without expectation is idle wishing or dreaming. You simply waste much valuable energy in doing this. - Raymond Holliwell

---

As long as your desires do not interfere with the free will of another, there is no reason why you should not receive the good that you desire in THIS life. What it takes is your courage, confidence, belief and persistence. Wishing and hoping will not do a single thing but lead you to despair and rage. BELIEF and EXPECTATION must replace wishing and hoping.

And when you EXPECT something, what do you do? You PREPARE for whatever it is you are expecting. This is a tremendous energetic act of faith which can move mountains. An "expectant" parent will create a nursery or space with the supplies and bedding which are needed for the arrival of the baby. For the most part, your journey can be quantified in such precise timing as the nine months of gestation before the birth of a human baby. Therefore, you would do well to be ready to receive your good every moment of every day.

Check in with yourself. Are you READY TODAY for your expanding good? Or are you hemming and hawing and wishing and hoping that some "miracle" might happen today (or soon) which will bring all your dreams to fruition? It will not. It cannot. ONLY what you are a vibrational match to

CAN happen. Preparation and expecting helps you become a vibrational match to your desires.

If you KNEW your manifestation was coming within the next week, what would you DO to prepare for the arrival?

Money Magic Mantra:

I am preparing for the fulfillment of my vision because I know it is in the process of manifesting in my world!

DAY 53: I REMEMBER THE DAYS WHEN I WAS NOT RICH AND PROSPEROUS!

I remember when this just was an empty lot.
- Neville Goddard

Through your vibration, your Consciousness, you are summoning your good or your lack, for this is a vibrational attraction-based universe. Therefore, it is your vibration which must be changed even more than your behavior. Whatever is in your consciousness is what you are getting more of in your personal world. Change your consciousness and you change your world.

There is a game the great mystic Neville Goddard taught his students which is the *"I remember when"* game. It is a way to move to the consciousness of ALREADY HAVING the good you desire. And when you are in that consciousness, you become irresistible to whatever vibrates at that same frequency.

Neville told the story of a man who would stand with his sons on an empty lot and say, *"I remember when this was just an empty lot before we built our beautiful mansion with all the blah, blah, blah"* (filling in all the details of the home that at the time they had no money to build or even break ground on). He would get into the vision and the WONDERFUL FEELING of the vision already completed without having any idea HOW it would ever happen. And yet happen it did because this man knew how the LAWS OF CONSCIOUSNESS OPERATE. He knew how to RELAX and summon his good to him in the same way many others summon catastrophe and struggle. If you do it properly, it is a very FUN game to play.

Try it out and see for yourself if it does not shift your consciousness to a much better-feeling place. But make sure you are not just saying "I remember when things were harder" - you must FILL IN THE NEW experience and vision that you WANT to take the place of the old limitation. Fill it in JOYOUSLY without outlining in any way HOW it happened. How is not your part. Having FUN is your part.

<u>Money Magic Mantra</u>:

I remember when I didn't have all this money left over after paying all my bills!

DAY 54: I EASILY MEET EVERY NEED WITH PLENTY LEFT OVER TO SPARE AND TO SHARE.

I have known people who had a definite prosperity consciousness for years, who were able to live comfortably, easily and with freedom. They did not let major money problems bother them. Little negatives of lack, however, crept into their consciousness. Where formerly they looked at the newspaper and said, "Another tax? All right, I'll make more money and pay it," now they sit back and complain, "Another tax? Someone should change the administration!" Gradually they have allowed a negative to build in their minds until it becomes a block to their success.
- Raymond Charles Barker

You absolutely MUST post a guard at the door of your mind to keep all the nonsense and negativity of the world from poisoning your consciousness with fear, lack and limitation. This is why We always advise humans to avoid the "news" as much as possible. It is not "new" in the least. It is the same old, same old since time began and practically the ONLY thing reported is the "bad" news.

In fact, the good news SO entirely outweighs the bad as to be hilarious! A 24 hour "news" channel that reported only good news would be of no interest to 99.99999% of humans but they would have so much good news even locally that not even a fraction of one town could cover their own local "good" news. If they covered everyone who fell in love that day, got a raise, made a child laugh, healed a cut, forgave another, grew their own tomatoes, gave and received presents, helped a neighbor, and on and on - well, it would be IMPOSSIBLE to report the ENDLESS OVERWHELMING GOOD that is happening everywhere on earth ALL THE TIME. It's simply that few would be interested, and it would not sell products because the sale of most products is fear-based. "You NEED this!"

Therefore, you must guard your mind and not let the world take a dump in it. You must not let in the seemingly "little" negatives for they will invite in their friends for a party and will trash your mental house until it is a disaster area. If you guard your mind in this way, when seemingly "bad" news comes you will say, "Oh, no need to worry, I always have what I need whenever I need it - with plenty left over to share and to spare!"

<u>Money Magic Mantra</u>:

Something wonderful and prosperous is happening for me today - and every day!

DAY 55: PROSPERITY IS MY DIVINE RIGHT.

The Lord is my banker; my credit is good. He maketh me to lie down in the consciousness of omnipresent abundance; He giveth me the key to His strongbox. He restoreth my faith in His riches; He guideth me in the paths of prosperity for His name's sake . . . Thou preparest a way for me in the presence of my collector; Thou fillest my wallet with plenty; my measure runneth over. - Charles Fillmore

---

As the rain falls on the just and the unjust, it should be clear to you by now that no good is being withheld from anyone and that there is nothing "unspiritual" about money and prosperity. It is the good pleasure of your Divine Source to pour out limitless blessings and good upon all who OPEN UP to receive the gifts of the Universe.

It is a very good practice very morning to stand up strong, throw your arms open wide and say aloud, "I open to receive the gifts of the Universe today! I open to receive the blessings of Source!" Say this 3 times aloud and really FEEL yourself opening to receive - not to "get" but to receive. The word "get" usually creates a kind of grasping mental energy which is not the same as receiving. There is no need to go outside and GET some rain - simply let it fall on you as you receive the cooling cleansing waters. This is the attitude to cultivate in terms of your prosperity. You are not GETTING it but simply opening to receive it.

Money Magic Mantra:

I open to receive the gifts of the Universe today. I open to receive the blessings of Source.

DAY 56: I AM THE KIND OF PERSON WHO IS ALWAYS PROSPERING AND THRIVING FINANCIALLY.

We could relieve ourselves of a vast load of care, anxiety and worry, if we could but recognize the simple truth, that our Creator made ample provisions for us to live successfully in this or any other age by providing us with a built-in creative mechanism. - Maxwell Maltz

---

Indeed, you are endowed by Source with a built-in creative mechanism which is always creating whatever it is that is in alignment with your SELF-CONCEPT. Your self-concept is even more important than what you think about money, prosperity, how the world works and even what Source is. You live the life of the person you BELIEVE yourself to be. If you see yourself as a failure or as one who must always struggle, that will be your experience no matter what opportunities come your way. If you want to change your experience, you must change your self-concept.

This is why "I AM" is such an important start to any sentence - whatever you complete that sentence with is actually prophesying your future. The built-in creative mechanism is forever responding to YOUR words and thoughts - the stories you tell yourself ABOUT yourself. This is why it is so important to pay attention to what you say TO YOURSELF ABOUT YOURSELF! If you see yourself as pitiful, you will be pitiful. If you see yourself as powerful, you will be powerful. It is very simple, but simplicity is very difficult for twisted minds.

We strongly suggest you get centered and quiet, and then write out a list in which you HONESTLY evaluate the kind of person YOU think you are - not what others tell you, but what you HONESTLY think. It should start with something like, "I am the kind of person who . . . " and keep on completing that sentence. You can do this over several days or weeks. Keep noticing which concepts are lifting you up, and which ones are keeping you down. Then know you can CHOOSE to change the ones that no longer serve you. Turn them around to the opposite and make them a dominant daily Money Magic Mantra which you say aloud 7 times every morning. This is Our prescription for shifting your Consciousness to a better feeling place.

<u>Money Magic Mantra</u>:

I am the kind of person who easily makes positive changes.

DAY 57: I AM WORTHY AS FUCK!

Again, nothing you think or wish or make is necessary to establish your worth. - A Course in Miracles

---

Of course, feel free to change that to, "I am worthy AF" if that suits your personality better. But We wanted it to be very STRONG for you to OWN this vibration because it is truly EVERYTHING that this course has been about all along. If you can really accept this truth, then prosperity is yours and will always be yours. This is your core work now and forevermore in this physical vibrational Universe. Know and accept your worthiness and you ARE a Master of Manifesting your visions.

In fact, YOU are your own master demonstration. Prosperity is not about demonstrating money and things, but rather is about manifesting YOU as your most authentic fabulous self. When you are doing that, money and things will flow to you freely and blessings with hang onto you like static cling on nylon.

We've been leading you along this journey to get you to this point of outrageous but true DECLARATION that you are WORTHY AS FUCK! We would like that to be your own little sacred mantra that you carry in your heart every day of your life. It will not do you much good if you are open to receive but still do not believe you are TOTALLY WORTHY to receive the good that comes. You'll just sabotage it or fuck it up or give it all away or reject it or it will only last a season. That is not what this course is about. This course is about permanent stable and ever-increasing prosperity - and that is wholly dependent on your knowing your worthiness. Put it on a post-it, get it on a tattoo, write it on the bathroom mirror or do whatever in order to have this thought foremost in your mind from this point forward.

Money Magic Mantra:

I am worthy as fuck, and I am open to receive all the gifts and riches of the Universe in all the forms that will bring the most joy!

DAY 58: I AM VALUABLE AND HAVE SOMETHING WORTHY TO CONTRIBUTE.

Determine exactly what you intend to give in return for the money you desire. (There is no such reality as "something for nothing.") - Napoleon Hill, Think and Grow Rich

---

While there is no need to struggle and suffer in order to prosper, just wanting to sit around being rich is not part of the Universal Plan of joyous expansion. It defies the law of circulation. In fact, many who retire and start sitting around have strokes or succumb to dementia because they are no longer circulating energy and are slowly withering away. Their minds are not busy CREATING something positive and life-giving so that mind begins to die off or begins creating negatively.

Just wanting to be "rich" without providing something in return is mere idle wishing and will not activate much of a magnetic charge. Find something that you love or that brings you JOY and begin doing it and sharing it. Do NOT think of it in terms of a "job" or career so much as a contribution in the law of circulation. Do not make it something you "should" be doing, particularly if it does not FEEL GOOD to you. FEELING GOOD is the primary thing here, for that will be the magnetic force for attracting prosperity to you. This is not about a "paying gig" but rather an energy exchange. You will do this thing and money will flow to you, but not necessarily from that thing you are doing - do you see? YOU must put OUT the energy of joyous contribution and then be willing and expecting to receive, but from ANYWHERE, not necessarily from the thing you are doing or contributing. You may have a passionate love for growing tomatoes and then canning them and giving them to everyone in the neighborhood. Even that will stimulate prosperity if you do it with the right Consciousness.

This has nothing to do with charitable giving or "service" work. It is about circulation. As soon as you stop contributing to life, your body, mind and spirit will start to wither for you have cut off the circulation. If you cut off circulation to your arm, it will wither and die. Circulation is life. Congestion is dis-ease and death. It is law.

<u>Money Magic Mantra</u>:

As I share what I love, money flows to me in great abundance!

DAY 59: I GET TO LIVE MY DREAMS JUST BECAUSE I DO.

Delight yourself in the Lord and he will give you the desires of your heart. - Psalm 37:4

And the Lord is the Divine in YOU! Delight yourself in this glorious magical mystical inner Presence and allow It to give you the desires of your heart. You are not petitioning an entity far away up in the clouds to please, please, please, pretty please do you a big FAVOR and allow you to have a fabulous life. You are only ever convincing YOURSELF. IF you need to do a sales pitch, it is always, always, always to your own subconscious mind! So, never try to justify why you want the life you want. It is YOUR life, your decision to make. As long as you are not hurting another or yourself, go for it baby!

If necessary, write yourself out a "permission slip" that you are ALLOWED to live the life of your dreams, just because you say so. Period. In fact, YOU are the only one who needs to believe in your dreams or believe in YOU. And the more you do, the more you will attract others who mirror that belief.

Money Magic Mantra:

I have nothing to prove to anyone. I give myself permission to be, do and have the life I choose simply because I want to.

DAY 60: I CANNOT OUT-GIVE THE UNIVERSE!

Bring all the tithe into the storehouse, that there may be food
in my house. Test me in this, "says the LORD Almighty,
"and see if I will not throw open the floodgates of heaven
and pour out so much blessing that there will not be room
enough to store it. - Malachi 10

The word "tithe" means a tenth. To tithe is to give 10 percent
of your income to support whatever or whoever spiritually
feeds you. It MAY be a church or religious organization but
often is not. It is any person or organization or group from
which you receive spiritual food. It is not done as a means to
get a tax break but as a sowing of seed financially. What you
sow, you will reap. If you donate your time and service you
will reap time and service. If you want to reap money, you
must sow money in the same way that a watermelon seed
will only grow watermelons.

Charitable giving to "need" is not a tithe, that is "alms
giving" and should be over and above a tithe and is a
wonderful thing. Anything less than 10% is still giving but is
not a tithe. Giving to needy friends and relatives is not
tithing but is also alms giving.

Tithing is for those who want to turbo-charge their
prosperity. We end this book with this lesson for those of
you who are eager for more and want to take your prosperity
to the next level. But be sure to do your best to be a
JOYOUS giver and that you do it EXPECTING to
RECEIVE. BLESS your tithe AS you give it. Do not do this
unconsciously but CONSCIOUSLY and care as you would

planting a summer garden. You plant a garden JOYOUSLY by GIVING seeds to the earth and letting them go. And you EXPECT a plant to grow as long as you weed and water and plant in the right soil. There is nothing unspiritual about tithing and EXPECTING to have a financial increase return blessed and multiplied any more than you would be wrong for planting one apple seed and expecting many apples to come forth from the tree when it is mature.

And now, We say "Amen" and go with you to guide you individually every time you turn within seeking such guidance. There is great abundance and great prosperous good for you if you will do the inner Consciousness work to OPEN TO RECEIVE! We love you.

<u>Money Magic Mantra</u>:

My giving makes me rich!

Notes

SUGGESTED READING:

The 4 Spiritual Laws of Prosperity
Edwene Gaines

The Dynamic Laws of Prosperity
Catherine Ponder

Prosperity
Charles Fillmore

The Little Money Bible
Stuart Wilde

Health, Joy and Prosperity for YOU!
Reverend Ike

The Master Key System
Charles F. Haanel

The Science of Getting Rich
Wallace D. Wattles

The Science of Successful Living
Raymond Charles Barker

The Law and the Promise
Neville Goddard

Jacob Glass is an author, spiritual teacher, mentor and international supermodel. To order his other books, see his live class schedule or receive his weekly class recordings, see his website jacobglass.com

Printed in Great Britain
by Amazon